SOLUTION-CENTER
SOCIOLOG

SOLUTION-CENTERED SOCIOLOGY

Addressing

Problems

Through

Applied

Sociology

Stephen F. Steele

AnneMarie Scarisbrick-Hauser

William J. Hauser

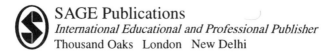

SAGE Publications
International Educational and Professional Publisher
Thousand Oaks   London   New Delhi

For information:

SAGE Publications, Inc.
2455 Teller Road
Thousand Oaks, California 91320
E-mail: order@sagepub.com

SAGE Publications Ltd.
6 Bonhill Street
London EC2A 4PU
United Kingdom

SAGE Publications India Pvt. Ltd.
M-32 Market
Greater Kailash I
New Delhi 110 048 India

Printed in the United States of America

Library of Congress Cataloging-in-Publication Data

Steele, Stephen F.
   Solution-centered sociology: Addressing problems through applied sociology / by Stephen F. Steele, AnneMarie Scarisbrick-Hauser, William J. Hauser.
      p. cm.
   Includes bibliographical references and index.
   ISBN 0-7619-1351-3 (cloth : acid-free paper)
   ISBN 0-7619-1352-1 (pbk. : acid-free paper)
   1. Applied sociology. I. Scarisbrick-Hauser, AnneMarie. II. Hauser, William J. III. Title.
   HN29.5 .S74 1998
   301--ddc21   98-25413

This book is printed on acid-free paper.

   00 01 02 03 10 9 8 7 6 5 4 3 2

Acquiring Editor:	Peter Labella
Editorial Assistant:	Renée Piernot
Production Editor:	Sherrise M. Roehr
Editorial Assistant:	Stephanie Allen
Typesetter/Designer:	Rose Tylak
Cover Designer:	Candice Harman

This book is dedicated to Cindy, Scott, and Matt Steele, who all know the wonder and the value of understanding human interaction, and to Erik Hauser, who for many years has asked his parents what a sociologist does for a living. We hope this book answers those questions.

Contents

Part III: Curtain Call

Part IV: Taking the Show on the Road

Preface

During this past century, the discipline of sociology has taken on many shapes and forms. At times in its history, sociology has focused on the "basic" study of groups and societies, attempting to better understand how they are defined, are developed, and interact in an ever-changing, complex social environment. At other times, sociology has focused on the practical application of its knowledge and expertise to find solutions for a myriad of problems facing groups, communities, and societies. As the new millennium approaches, sociology is faced with a number of issues that challenge its relevancy to the 21st century and the problems that it will face in the future. This future will call upon the social sciences, and sociology, by its very nature, must be the leader in this endeavor. Thus, the pendulum appears to be swinging back toward the applied face of sociology.

In its purest sense, applied sociology is "doing" sociology. It is taking the theoretical models and the methodological techniques and using them in social situations to resolve problems or improve the quality of life, be it the challenge of macrolevel societal problems or microlevel, everyday personal issues. Because problem solving requires a number of approaches and perspectives, it is extremely hard to place applied sociology into one area of expertise. Today, applied sociology crosses a number of dimensions. It is a way of taking many of the areas of the sociological endeavor and giving them real-world applications. Through its involvement with a wide assortment of community, business, and governmental audiences, applied sociology provides the discipline with opportunities for further growth and development. It is also a way for students to view and better understand the foundations of the discipline and its practical uses in their own unique social environments.

Therefore, applied sociology is not one of a multitude of expertise areas in the domain of sociology. Instead, it is a unique core competency of the discipline. As such, the whole discipline becomes more fully integrated. Theories and models are developed and tested through the application of research techniques in a real-world social laboratory. In turn, the results are used to develop and implement practical solutions to social situations and problems. The evaluation of these solutions is, in fact, an evaluation of the principles and techniques of sociology. The integration of this process moves sociology forward.

This book has been written to serve a number of purposes. First, it gives you, the student, an applied view of numerous social factors that are part of your daily life. Second, the book offers a number of tools that you can use to better understand and inform others about the complex array of social events, attitudes, and activities that are a part of the social environment. Finally, the book is constructed as a ready reference and toolkit that you can repeatedly draw upon as you apply your sociological skills at work, school, or as part of your normal day-to-day interaction.

The authors of this book require one thing of you. This book cannot be read and then filed away on some dusty bookshelf. It must be used! You must continually draw upon it as a toolkit to help you view your social world and continue to develop your storehouse of practical uses of sociology.

Acknowledgments

The authors gratefully acknowledge a number of individuals who have helped to bring this book to fruition. We would like to thank Joyce Iutcovich for her input on some of the early chapter composition. We would also like to thank Teri Kepner for her editing and preparation of the final manuscript. Special appreciation goes to the reviewers whose suggestions have helped to make the book more complete. Finally, we would like to thank Peter Labella and the staff at Sage Publications for all of their valuable assistance.

PART  I

Setting the Stage

A World of Problems

Why a book on using sociology to solve problems? As applied sociologists, we are convinced that using sociology can make a significant contribution to improving the quality of life. Undoubtedly, you are increasing your awareness of the value of the sociological perspective to view the world around you. But, at the same time, you may have shared a similar reaction with others who have said, "It's fascinating stuff, but what can I do with it?" Using this book as a resource, we think that you will be able to move from the fascinating to the functional, from the philosophical to the practical.

Applied sociologists tend to look at things differently from the more traditional sociologists. All sociologists are trained to do research, much of it basic. Basic research is testing a theory to validate, improve, or reject it. Classic theorist Emile Durkheim encouraged the application of knowledge to real problems. So, when he wrote *Suicide* (1951), he may well have been personally concerned about the problem of suicide itself. In the minds of contemporary theorists, however, his primary interest in the book appears to be a test of a theory. From a basic research view, he was interested in using data on suicide in Europe to test a theory concerning integration in society. In basic scientific research, whether in sociology, psychology, biology, or chemistry, the "theory" is the problem. That is, what we want to know is whether the theoretical road map is an accurate one.

This can be good news and bad news. Sociologists are trained and rewarded for understanding and expanding theories of society. Theories are important, and good theories make good practice possible. How can one act effectively on something if he or she does not know

3

how it works? So, the good news is that basic research in sociology is important and should be fully utilized and developed. On the other hand, many sociologists who teach the discipline (and, therefore, many of the students who learn sociology) follow a basic research perspective. Traditionally, students who become sociology majors are often confined to this approach. The bad news is that they end up "cloning" the perspective, and the basic research philosophy perpetuates itself. The bad news gets even worse when students attempt to take their sociology out of the basic setting and use it, only to eventually disappear (they do not call themselves sociologists anymore and do not identify with the field). Most importantly, they do not feed back important information that might have an impact on improving sociology. Even worse, some sociologists who apply their skills in business or government actually may be berated by mainstream sociologists.

Let us look at Emile Durkheim's *Suicide* another way. Suppose we view suicide as a real-world problem. Our concern is to do something about this problem: to understand and change the social forces that create this horrible situation that results in the end of a person's life. A client, such as a group of parents or a board of education, may ask the question: "Why is this happening to our children?" As sociologists, how do we go about identifying and understanding the factors that cause the problem, and how do we develop programs to help solve the problem? If we start out with this approach, the emphasis varies between an applied sociologist and a basic sociologist (see Figure 1.1).

How is it different? Let us look at three ways in which it is different. First, concern for the real-world problem is the focus of our attention. Applied sociologists passionately want to know how to *address and find solutions for* the suicide problem. Applying sociological skills and expertise to improve conditions is the first and foremost concern, and validating theories of suicide, although very important, is secondary. Second, applied sociologists draw on the skills, tools, and methods of sociology as resources that can be applied immediately. When a problem exists, there is usually little or no time to conduct a research project on the validity of the tool or process itself. The best tools must be selected and executed.

We do not want to use shoddy methods. Nor are we immediately interested in adding fuel to the fire of an academic debate about whether qualitative or quantitative methods are the most academically pure. Instead, we are more interested in using the best tools that fit the situation. This might mean key informant interviews in one situation,

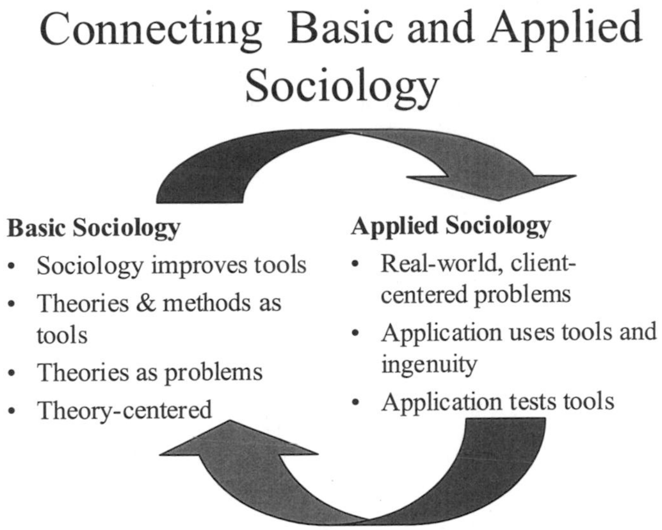

Connecting Basic and Applied Sociology

Basic Sociology

- Sociology improves tools
- Theories & methods as tools
- Theories as problems
- Theory-centered

Applied Sociology

- Real-world, client-centered problems
- Application uses tools and ingenuity
- Application tests tools

Figure 1.1 Connecting Basic and Applied Sociology

focus groups in another, or survey research in yet another. Likewise, to the applied sociologist, sociological concepts and theories are tools that may be used to improve our ability to grasp a real-world problem.

Finally, basic researchers often find themselves narrowing their focus on a single specialty. This makes sense; sociology is a broad discipline. Testing theories concerning specialty areas such as criminology or demography, for example, requires that you know as much as you can about the concepts and models in those areas. This is not to say that an applied sociologist cannot be a specialist; however, he or she is often likely to benefit from broadening the toolkit. This means learning as many new tools as possible, enhancing divergent rather than convergent thinking, and looking for creative ways to rigorously use the tools.

Let us take another real-life example. Some years ago, the police in a suburban county were confronted with a series of dreadful murders of local gas station attendants. The police asked for help in determining the nature of these crimes. Their interest was not on theories of homicide or validating theories of criminology. They simply wanted to know how they could address this real-world problem. Social science research was employed to assist. The key factor here was the emphasis and the response. Tools were brought to bear on the situation to solve a problem facing the community. Theories of suicide or crime were not neglected. Instead, they were actually tested in a real-life situation—not to test their validity but to apply their information to resolve a problem. As important as using the tools is reporting the outcome, so that others can apply similar strategies in related situations when they arise. There needs to be a "tension" between theory and practice. If the theories do not work in real settings, basic researchers need to "get back to the drawing board."

≋ What Can Sociology Add?

Most applied sociologists love what they do! The sociological perspective is a very effective orientation to use in a multitude of social situations and events. However, real-world problems are humbling in that applying what we know may be exhilaratingly comprehensive in one setting and embarrassingly inadequate in others. In a world of problems and problem solvers, we are better off asking: What can sociology *add* to understanding and solving the problem? What perspective and methods can we use to have more of an impact on a situation? Just what do sociologists bring to the table that can be used in dealing with and solving a problem? There are at least two answers to this question: perspectives and tools. Let us look at each.

There are countless pages in sociology texts devoted to the notion of the sociological perspective. This perspective is a view of the world that looks at social structures and social processes. When we look at social life, we begin to see *interactions, not people.* Sociology is grounded in the belief that "action-between" or "action-among" people produces the state of being in which we live. Consider another example. Suppose you are an independent consultant trying to enhance organizational development by using your sociological expertise. The local fire chief hires you and starts his conversation by saying: "People aren't what they used to be. They do not honor volunteering for their city or country anymore. The country is going to the dogs . . . people simply aren't as good as they were. Nobody will volunteer for the fire department."

This view is known as "blaming the person"; that is, bad people added up equal a bad society. As a sociologist, you will want to look at the chief's assessment a little differently. Sociologists are more likely to ask a variety of questions about the ways in which people in the society respond to this situation. For example, you will want to know what the current role sets look like for people who are likely volunteers. What groups of people are the most likely to volunteer? How is this role of firefighter currently defined? What is expected of volunteers in this role? Are there traditional sets of role expectations that make it impossible for some people to actually volunteer as firefighters? Sociologists will want to evaluate the answers to these and other questions and then develop some reasons as to why people do not volunteer to be firefighters.

This leads us to a second unique view. Sociologists are constantly looking at situations. For most of us, it is difficult to sort out individual behavior and emotions from the situations that caused them. This is a role normally played by psychologists. However, there are very few situations in which any one of us operates in a vacuum (i.e., totally alone). We are almost always in a collective situation, whether it is real or perceived. Here is what we mean. For years, a local department store maintained a set of escalators located in the middle of the store. When a shopper entered the store and wanted to go to the second level, the escalators were in clear sight. No doubt an architect had positioned them so that there would be no confusion as to how you get upstairs. The situation made sense until you got to the escalators themselves. We would expect to go to the right. Unfortunately, if you tried the right-hand escalators in this store, you might be surprised to find that the right escalator stairs were going down. Clearly, a small inconvenience; yet more than likely, the reasoning behind putting the up escalator on the left, nearest the incoming door, was to improve the efficiency of the system. How efficient is a situation laid out this way? This was a situation laid out in contrast to a cultural definition. This would have been acceptable to a European but confusing to an American. This produces deviance, surprise, and perhaps a personal or psychological response. Thus, *real social situations* are causes that affect human choices and outcomes. We practice applied sociology when we look at the nature of social situations.

Perceived situations are often as real as the one just described. For the most part, we make up our worlds, and then we live in them. As cognitive creatures, we can bring into our social reality just about anybody we want: people long dead, people currently living whom we know or do not know, and people yet to exist. Here is an example. For years, two of the authors have worked with people who are grieving. Our goal was not to provide therapy but to understand how grievers understood and, as a result, dealt with their reality (you can see immediately how this becomes applied sociology). In self-help groups, grievers discussed their lives and the worlds in which they had and were currently living now that someone important had died. Death is a powerful force in revealing the existence and nature of the social fabric in which we live. Grief is the intersection of highly personal and unique human emotions with the socially created world in which we live. Grievers often have encounters with people who have died, not just through dreams but through perceived social rituals, such as flowers on one's birthday, finding a stuffed toy, or running into someone who "looked just like Dad." We become sensitive to the fact that we are tied into a socially defined self that is a two-way street. We make it up, and it is made up for us by others, and then we live in that world, that situation, that is in the making. As Berger and Luckmann (1966) say, we live within an ever-changing "social product."

▨ Defining an Applied Problem: How Do You Know One When You See One?

Defining problems is central to sociology. Unfortunately, it has been glossed over too often. When we are looking at an applied problem, we need to review at least three things: (a) the type of problem, (b) the level of analysis, and (c) possible sociological perspectives. Let us take these in turn.

If a real-world situation is viewed as a problem, it usually is for one of three reasons. First, the situation (and, hence, the interactions produced by the situation) is a discrepancy between the real and the ideal. Here is an example. A small business owner may lament that she cannot keep up with orders for her company's accounting software. No matter how hard her employees work, they cannot get enough orders out the door. As an applied sociologist, you could help here by viewing this situation as a discrepancy between the *social system* she has in place to fill orders and the volume of demand (the needs). We might just need to add more people, but the solution might involve restructuring—that is, reorganizing the situation—or, of course, changing demand. Notice how no one is blamed for the situation?

Another way to look at a problem is to view a situation as a clash of values between two or more groups. Not surprisingly, labor-management conflicts are common examples of this type of problem, but such a problem might be more subtle. For example, in a large company, a value clash may emerge from the "technological purity" values of the engineering department and the "get it out the door, deliver it on time" values of the sales department. The solutions are usually of two kinds here. One type of solution is to create a *synthesis:* some new way to value the situation or some constructed common ground to deal with the contrary views. Another approach would be to view some level of conflict as healthy, because the presence of conflict may suggest some underlying issue that needs resolution.

Finally, a problem may exist simply because a group of people has been able to get everyone to collectively define a situation that way. If this sounds circular (i.e., "it is because it is"), do not worry. We have had poverty, crime, and hunger with us for a long time, but our society does not always define them as problems. The solution may be in the defining or redefining of the situation.

Certainly, a situation that encompasses all three of these (a discrepancy between real and ideal, a value clash, and something defined as a problem) has vast credibility within a group. Although discrepancies often produce value clashes and/or become defined as problems, this is just not always the case. To adequately understand the problem, we may need to look at it in all of these ways, and perhaps in ways never before understood.

It is important here to try to determine the problem and reach a consensus between you and your client. This is essential. If you and your client are superficially agreeing (both "nodding your heads in the same direction," but neither of you has a "clue"), you're in for big trouble. Here's why. First, you'll study the wrong thing. This produces wasted time and effort, not to mention lost resources. Second, you may produce possible tension between you and your client. Both of you may honestly claim that you agreed on the problem, only to find that you are later accused of studying the wrong thing. Anger, anxiety, and embarrassment are all part of this outcome. It does not do much good to blame your client at that point. Remember that it is up to you to understand what the client means when he or she says there is a problem.

We like to think of problem definition as a "social construction of reality" (Berger & Luckmann, 1966). We know it is jargon, but it is good jargon! Look at the words. "Social" . . . more than one person, so we are working on something shared here; "construction" . . . creating or making, so you and your clients are jointly making something; "reality" . . . a thing, a place. By creating this "thing" on which we agree is a problem, and getting consensus on how we define it, we are on the way to some good sociological sailing. "Clients" are the people for whom we are working. Their understanding of the problem may span a broad spectrum, from no understanding at all to complete and thorough understanding. The fact remains that your reality and theirs cannot be separate. You begin to realize that problem definition is just plain hard work. It demands clear communication that is often iterative (i.e., talking about the situation over and over again). If you are working with a group of clients, this can require skills in group discussion and team problem identification.

⍰ Levels of Social Organization: Where's the Problem?

When we ask "Where is the problem?" a sociologist not only thinks about location in time and space but also considers its place in social space. Sociologists' responsibility lies with human interaction on a broad spectrum—from the person to the group (families, communities, organizations) to the society (cultures, institutions, the global village)! That is a fair amount of social ground to cover. As sociologist Linda Weber (1995) indicates, we work at *micro* (people, selves); *meso* (groups, communities); and *macro* (societies, cultures) levels. To understand a problem we need to locate it at one of these levels (p. 13). At the same time, we must avoid the arrogance of forgetting our colleagues in other fields who look at humans at the *suborganic* level, such as psychologists and biologists; as well as those who carve out pieces of the social condition, such as economists and political scientists. They all have something important to say, and their unique interpretations of situations are needed.

To make sense of a problem, finding its level is important. But where a problem surfaces is very likely to have both "within"-layer and "among"-layer characteristics. For example, the local elementary school begins to report unusual rates of absenteeism because of an outbreak of measles. The problem initially is a microlevel one in the sense that children interact person-to-person and pass illnesses from one to another. Clearly, solving this problem would require some microlevel interventions. This intervention works "within" a level of social organization. Are there meso and macro problems? At first glance, we are not sure. But in an applied view, we will want to look. What is this school's rate of infection in comparison to others around it? Others similar to it? Now we are thinking about mesolevel groups: schools.

How effective have local health systems been in vaccinating children for measles? Has social class had an impact on the vaccination of children? Again, meso. Finally, have federal cutbacks in health care or the introduction of a new federal system to distribute vaccinations had some impact here (macro)? The problem surfaces among individuals, within a micro layer of social organization, but we can trace it to meso and macro levels as well. And trace it we must. That is part of the "sociologist's burden." As a discipline, we are holistic—we look at the whole thing.

⚥ Tools of the Trade

Once a problem is identified and defined, applied sociologists need to do something about it. Sociological practitioners may be asked to work with problems for a variety of reasons—to know about it by researching it, on one hand, and to "fix it" by intervention, on the other hand. Regardless, we need tools. These tools usually fall in two groups: conceptual tools (concepts and theories, ways to know a problem) and methodological tools (ways to actively engage and/or research the problem). We will look at each of these.

In most sociology programs, theory courses are separated from methods courses. This suggests that there is a distinction between thinking and doing. Often, we get the impression that theories fall in the "wake me when it's over" category: memorize it, forget it, and then move on to the real action part—methods. Applied sociologists may have learned their theories and methods this way, but they do not have the luxury of separating them when they are addressing an applied problem. *How can you begin to solve a problem in a social system when you do not have the foggiest idea of how that system works?* For applied sociologists, there are tools and then there are *more* tools! Taking this approach, how can theories be used as tools?

A wide variety of theories exist in sociology. But there are at least three that currently stand out in the field: functionalism (or the systems paradigm, as Babbie calls it); conflict; and interactionism (Babbie, 1994). For the applied sociologist, the key ingredient is how they are applied. They can be used one at a time or all at once. Here is an example.

A local church may be seen as a system. The roles and statuses (minister, members of the congregation, church trustees, the lay leaders) may be seen as interdependent at a micro level. At a meso level, the religious education committee is interdependent with the church facilities committee. They are both dependent on the finance committee. The church as a whole is dependent on the community in which it is located. All in all, we see the church as a social phenomenon of interdependent, perhaps interlocking, parts. The church is a *structure*. Remember that *norms* (rules) are the building blocks of structures. When these organized blocks comprise some temporary formation to which people can attach themselves, we get structures. We link structures as individuals through roles. Structure depends on agreement that the rules exist and that they are legitimate. All of the structures, whether micro, meso, or macro, exist because they serve some function. In fact, the shape of the parts, even how the structures are organized, are based on the purpose that they serve for people, on one hand, and for other structures and social forces on the other hand. The system works toward some sort of equilibrium between need and structures in an evolving balancing act.

That is one view. Now, we will look at it from another perspective. We can see the church as a collection of centers of power. The committees in the church, as well as roles and statuses and the people who maintain them, have vested, established interests in maintaining these positions or groups. Layers emerge in the church based on a belief that the powerful will remain that way and that there is little anyone can do to rectify this imbalance. The powerful groups pretty much get what they want. For change to occur, a "consciousness of exploitation," followed by conflict, must occur. The result will be a *synthesis*, something new, not necessarily like that which went before.

Finally, the church is a *collective definition of reality* shared by a group of people. It is not only a religious belief system that many people share, but it is also a set of ways of living and seeing the world. In this sense, the roles, beliefs, and values, as well as the way people do things, are part of corporate culture (Schein, 1992). Sacred symbols, rituals, and roles are all maintained by definition and the maintenance of these definitions in everything from church school to the church bazaar. Change comes from the redefinition of reality.

None of us wants you to stop with our rather basic views of the applications of these theories to a social situation. Studying theory is a lifelong pursuit. But now, let us just see what happens when the church has a problem. Suppose the church is faced with a problem of whether it should invest in a larger building. Church leaders come to you because, as a sociologist, you should have some insights into these things!

Using sociological theory can be extremely valuable in moving toward sizing up the problem, even if you know very little about churches or religion in general. Which of the three theories should you use? Use all three!

First, view the church as a *social system* that processes people. It has an internal structure, both social and physical, for doing this. Furthermore, it is part of a larger social system (meso) in the area it serves and in the society (macro) in which it resides. What is the nature of the current system? What are its parts? How are they organized? What needs are currently served? How well does the church currently process people and serve needs? This list of questions emerges immediately if you view the church as a system. So, as you can see, the church is a system (functionalist theory).

At the same time, start looking for the church "power centers": groups of people and structures that tend to control church resources, people, and activities. Sometimes, these will not be obvious. For example, you expect the church clergy to be powerful, but the true power may reside in a long-time church benefactor who has been making contributions to the church's well-being for years. This person may not be so obvious. So, the church is a collection of people with power and vested interests (conflict theory).

Simultaneously, the church's existence is based on formal and informal ways of life. Decision-making processes, ways of dealing with problems, and who should be involved in those problems are based on the corporate culture of the church. At the same time, the religious faith supported by the church membership sets the tone for church activity. You need to understand this unique way of seeing the world to the best of your ability. You may not agree with it, but if you are to solve the problem, you must understand it. So, the church is a corporate culture with a set of shared symbols (interaction theory).

By now, the point is clear: Use all of your tools! This is true for two reasons. First, by methodically working through the situation using each perspective, you provide a more comprehensive view of the situation, and you are less likely to miss something. Second, you are less likely to be surprised. The minute you focus only on a systems perspective, powerful people will pop up. Likewise, the minute you understand the symbolic world of the church, social system forces (e.g., changing demographics) may emerge.

Now, we will turn our attention to the methodological tools. The tool selection process has at least five steps. First, *revisit the problem*. We cannot emphasize enough the importance of knowing the nature of the problem. Second, select a methodological tool or tools that fit the problem, not the other way around! You may develop a "pet" process (e.g., sociologists are known for their use of surveys, so everything gets surveyed), but this can develop a one-size-fits-all approach. Simply stated, one tool is too confining. In applied work, your goal is to expand your toolkit. You want to master as many tools as you can. Your goal is to use tools that give the best reliable and valid information possible. We arbitrarily break these into two groups: process tools and research tools.

Third, apply the tools to the problem. It makes sense, but this may be very revealing. Suppose the tools are inadequate for the problem. Suppose you plan to assist a local hospital that wants to know if it has an image problem in the community. You figure that a sample survey of the community makes sense (Tool #1). But suppose you find out that certain groups in the community have concerns with the hospital's emergency services. Your survey "radar" picked up the problem as a "blip on the screen." But how will you know what this means? Plan some focus groups (Tool #2) in preparation for this. When you bring your results to the board of directors at the hospital, a reasonable question might be, "What should we do to improve this situation?" If your clients trust you, they will likely ask. You might not know much about community hospitals, but you can respect the knowledge that your clients have and perhaps lead them in a brainstorming session (Tool #3), which might include nominal group technique (Tool #4).

Fourth, if the tool does not work, try another one. This suggests two things. First, you should not become dependent on one method. Versatility and ingenuity are central in applied work. Second, learn as many tools from as many sources as possible. This is lifelong learning, and it makes applied work a craft. Start with the tools you have, and grow in every way possible.

Fifth, and finally, do not be afraid to admit that you do not know how to do something. This will send you to a "quick study," on one hand, or to a colleague who has this skill (and please remember that this does not need to be a sociologist) on the other. You may need assistance, and you should not be afraid to get it. You will be able to find references to skills books and references that will help you to use each of the tools. We listed many of the tools in Appendix C in an annotated list with some examples of procedures so that you can get started now. For some of the tools, we have outlined the process in "cookbook" fashion. For

others, we have provided citations for references that will be very helpful. You may want to make some of them part of your toolkit.

Normally, you cannot get all of these tools in a standard academic
sociology curriculum. So get outside of sociology and look around.
Sociologists do not have a corner on the market for tools. Applied sociologists must constantly be on the alert for new tools, and then they
must learn them and incorporate them into their toolkit. Market research, economics, psychology, anthropology, human resources, and
organizational development are just a few of the fields that can provide
great tools. Remember, you cannot fully learn these tools unless you
use them! It will be absolutely essential that you wrestle with some of
the tools. Try them out in a safe environment, such as a training site or
classroom. Then, practice, practice, practice.

§ What Follows: Organization of Chapters

Each of the following chapters is set up so that you can work from
a sociological idea, a *concept*, to actually applying the idea in an applied
setting. We will go beyond the concepts to outline the expected actions
you will need to take and the outcomes that you can expect. In addition
to being a textbook that you might use in most classes on applied sociology, we would like this book to be a toolkit that you will plan to keep
with you as you practice your profession. So, in each chapter, you'll
find several useful ingredients for now and the future. Specifically,
you'll find the following:

1. *An action title.* We are serious. The titles should do two things: inspire
   you to act and, of course, serve as a recipe heading in an applied "cookbook." We hope these chapters get dog-eared as you use them over the
   years.
2. *Sociological key concepts.* Remember, we think concepts are tools. It is difficult to learn all of the tools at once. Furthermore, it is a rare situation
   that does not call for far more of the concepts than we will introduce in
   each chapter. For ease of learning, we will just introduce a few key concepts at a time, define them, and then put them to work! We hope that
   when you are finished, you will be able to put them all together.
3. *Sociologist as expert.* This section includes a brief discussion of why sociologists have the unique expertise and skills to study and provide solutions to the problem.

4. *Research tools.* In each chapter, we will introduce you to several tools that you could use to get hold of a problem of the kind that you might find in this chapter. We hope you will be putting these in your toolkit and that the kit will only expand: the more tools, properly understood, the better off you are.

5. *Presentation tools.* Why collect information if you cannot convey what you have found to your client? In an applied situation, your clients may come from a variety of backgrounds, education levels, and cultures. Writing research reports might be useful in some situations, but in many others, they could be downright offensive! At worst, they would be offensive and useless!! We will provide examples of a variety of tools for presenting information as we travel across the chapters.

6. *Case and solution.* In each chapter, we will provide a case study. This will be a real-life situation in which applied sociology could be used. We, of course, will ask you to use the tools we have presented in the chapter (and perhaps elsewhere) to the case. We will do the same, and then we will ask you to compare.

7. *Exercises.* Finally, we want you to get into the field and "do something." So, each chapter will include exercises. The exercise will work three ways. First, it will be yet another tool that you can use in an applied setting. Second, you will get a chance to see that talking sociology and applying sociology vary widely in their degrees of difficulty. Finally, the results of your exercises should be kept in a portfolio. We are convinced that many of these exercises will make you more employable and certainly more versatile in problem solving. As you complete the exercises in this book, we suggest that you store them in your own personal applied sociology portfolio. Keeping these exercises organized and readily accessible can be beneficial to you in a number of ways. First, the exercises are good examples of the types of work/projects that you successfully completed in school that can be shown to potential employers as part of the interview process. Most prospective employers like to see examples of the work that the job candidates have done. Second, the exercises filed in the applied sociology portfolio serve as handy references as you begin to tackle similar problems or issues in the workplace. Finally, without really thinking about it, you have created a substantial body of work in applied sociology that should make your numerous tasks in the future easier.

ᛦ Exercise

One of the most difficult tasks in the research act is clearly determining the problem to be researched. In this exercise, you must deal with this task.

Instructions:

1. *Client selection.* Select a person who might find an applied research project valuable. Such people will probably be in managerial roles in their respective organizations. Some examples would be the following:

- Business—department or division managers, personnel managers, market research managers, product research and development managers, long-range planning or forecasting personnel
- Government—department or division heads in city, state, or local government (all major departments apply; do not forget police and fire)
- Religion—local clergy; regional managers (bishops, local denominational personnel); lay governing boards
- Nonprofit organizations—boards of directors for everything from youth sports leagues to "body parts" organizations! Do not forget neighborhood associations.
- Education—principals, PTAs/PTOs, school board managers/members, college deans or academic department heads, teachers
- Political—political party leaders, local politicians and organizers

Of course, this is an incomplete list. Use your imagination. You might find that selecting a client poses some difficulty. Consult local directories of nonprofit organizations, business directories from the chamber of commerce, the telephone book for churches and political parties. Of course, the Internet can be a helpful resource here also. Volunteer organizations particularly have needs, and you can make an extraordinary contribution to these clients.

After you have selected a client, schedule a 1-hour session with this person. Explain in advance that you are doing this as part of a class.

2. *Conduct an interview session.* Interview your client. Strive to determine the following:

- What are the general research needs of this person? Try to develop a priority list of categories of research needs. Which of these needs reflects an evaluation project?
- What specific program does the client wish to have researched? What are the program goals? What are the measurable objectives? Get your client to identify the successful outcomes.
- Draw up a specific statement of the evaluation need and make a rough oral presentation of your estimation of the need. Seek clarification. Sometimes, this may be aided by saying, "When the research is done and the report written, what, specifically, do you want to know about [state research topic]? What do you really want researched?"

3. *Written assignment.* Provide the following written items for this class:

- Write a "thank you" business letter to your client. In the second paragraph of the letter, outline the research questions in a statement that resembles the following: "My interpretation of our discussion of your evaluation research needs revealed the following research questions:"

  _____?
  _____?

  Do not write more than one page!
- Send the original to your client and provide a copy for class review.

When Structure Is the Problem

Sociologists spend a great deal of time talking about structure. Contemporary life is full of businesses, schools, hospitals, and any number of social organizations that claim to be "re"structuring. If you think social structure is something that sociologists mention often but do not clarify, you are with us! This is another good example of how a little bit of sociology can be a powerful tool. Let us spend some time considering just what structure is and how it comes about.

We often say that a building is a structure, and that may be a good place to start our definition when we start thinking about applying the concept to social life. If a building is a structure, it has a number of characteristics. It is "something," it exists in reality. It has form or a shape to it. Furthermore, it is an organized set of building materials that, taken together, produce a thing. Once the building is complete, it sets the broad domain for what is to occur within it. For example, the size and shape of an airplane hangar built to house a 747 could accommodate a variety of activities. Some of these activities are relative to the purpose for which the building was intended (housing and repairing airplanes). Other activities seem to have little to do with the intended purpose (having a baseball game inside). The structure works well when it fits the need or the purpose for which it was created.

Social structure may be seen in a similar way. For example, a family with two parents (often married) and some children, let us say two for now, constitutes a structure. The family is a group, but right now we want to know how it is put together. Let us use some of the elements of structure that we mentioned in our building example. First, let us think of the family as a real-world thing. Social structures are *reifications*. (We do not want to bog you down with Latin, but here it makes sense: *reus* [thing] and the verb *faceo* [to make] = to make thinglike!) When we talk about "our family," we may talk about it as if it were a thing. In fact, for all practical purposes, families *are* bigger than the individuals in them, and they become entities unto themselves. When a family member does something for the good of the family, that human action is in response to something bigger than the individuals in the group. In some respects, this may be a response to the way this family is organized (its structure). Like a building, it may set the broad limits for things that you can do. In other words, the values, norms, roles, and systems of sanctions that support them actually seem to act as iron bars that can imprison or at least restrict the freedom of people. That is pretty "real" sounding! We do not want to ignore the people in the structure, but for now, we are trying to emphasize the importance of seeing structure as something real and separate from "individuals added up."

Second, social structures emerge as shapes or forms. We all know the problem of fitting a square peg into a round hole. Generally, it does not fit! When we expect social structures that were constructed to perform a certain set of tasks to respond to an entirely different set of tasks, we run into the same situation. Sometimes, in our circle/square example, we can get the square to fit by rounding off the edges of the square or by making the circle bigger. Regardless, we get a mismatch. A comparable example can be made if we were to expect our nuclear family to support itself by clearing with an axe and farming hundreds of acres of land with 18th-century equipment. We run into similar structural problems when we expect modern women to stay home with their children. Structural relationships between the family and other social structures (form and shape) may be at odds with one another. Notice that we are not talking about personal choice here; rather, we are emphasizing the way in which social forms have emerged.

George Ritzer (1996) presents the other side of this fit. The nuclear family is well adapted to the "McDonaldized" social forms that Ritzer describes in First World societies. Fast food, served rapidly in drive-through express lanes, is a formed complement to small structures (i.e., nuclear family). Small groups are able to move more rapidly and adapt rapidly to micro changes. On the other hand, they do not necessarily have the continuity and complexity to deal with large-scale change without higher levels of reliance on other structures in the system.

Third, and related to our previous comment, structure is organized. A structure's parts exist in some ordered arrangement. By this we mean that people progress through the structure along paths defined by the interlocking set of norms, values, and roles within. This system is often laid out and arranged in time and space (even when "space" means cyberspace). Furthermore, the external limits of the structure produce boundaries. Those inside and outside our family, those inside and outside our company, our church, and our country, for example, all demonstrate the limits of structural boundaries. Some structures have an input at one end and an output at the other end. In this way, they are "linear," or "nonrecursive." Sometimes, one can get in the structure simply by being born (ascribed roles and status). Other times, you can enter by choosing a place in the structure and then fulfilling the social requirements to maintain that place (achieved status and roles). For example, you can get "into" your family simply by being born.

In contrast, a company will have a structured path for hiring new employees. People seeking employment are interested in taking on the roles of those inside the company. To become an insider, one must move through the structured path of entrance. One progresses through the structure from new hire to retiree on an organized, socially determined path. This is not to suggest the image of the mindless robot. People have choices and varying levels of freedom, but the socially determined limits of choice and freedom are a function of collectively determined structure. The creativity of a research and development department in an organization, for example, demonstrates this point. People in the department may be wildly creative. New ideas abound, new worlds are created. Why? Because that is the function of the department: to find new information and develop it. Organizations that build in structures to foster creativity and employee imagination are likely to get it! A simple statement, but it is demonstrative of structure's role.

ⵉ How Does Structure Come About?

As we mentioned earlier in this book, there are primarily three sociological theoretical tools that explain how human social life unfolds. If we look at each of these, we get an explanation for just how social structure unfolds. We will look at these one at a time and then together, because we are better off if we can apply the tools in combination. But before we do, we will need to answer two questions. First, how does structure emerge? Once structure is in place, how does it act on the people who created it? Before long, you realize that we envision a continuous process.

How does structure emerge? If we use the interactionist tools, we know that we will need to get people together to create structure. Although this can be face to face, it does not need to be because virtual (Internet, even telephone) structures are as real as face-to-face structures. Through interaction (verbal and nonverbal), a two-person group will produce three realities. The reality for Person A, the reality for Person B, and, finally and importantly, a shared reality of A and B. In general, they will produce some definition couched in time and space (even if this is cyberspace). The outcome will be some norms (rules) for acting.

Remember, this is not Day 1 for humankind, so when people interact, there is already some structural baggage around. That is, some preexisting shared reality where norms are still maintained collectively. So, we rarely act in a social vacuum. There is always an atmosphere of structure, rules, and, hence, expectations for action. When humans interact, they often rely on the structure that is already present. They will bring their definitions of the structure into the situation, interact, and walk away with a new, slightly modified notion of the structure. If this is at a micro level (person to person), this may appear as an adjustment to the shared reality. It probably will not have an immediate major impact on the next level up (meso or macro). At least two things happen. First, we realize that this is a dynamic situation. The organized, ordered way that action occurs has changed a little bit, so some social change has occurred. Second, these changes are cumulative. We may see a long-term change in the meso and macro cultures as people collectively redefine the structure.

Now let us take a functionalist tool out of our toolkit. The structures we create are not going to survive very long if they do not perform functions or serve purposes: for us, for others, and for the *social system* itself! Now we have gone and done it! We have created something bigger than we are that needs care and feeding. This produces a system (another structure) of interacting worlds upon worlds. The people in the system need maintenance, and the system itself needs upkeep. Meso and macro structures are set up in such a way as to generally handle meso and macro problems. Microlevel systems adapt individuals for personal maintenance. Structure needs to "plug in" to human energy in order to make the system go. This occurs through the roles that humans take. Remember, roles are structures; hence, they are systems of norms that channel human potential into the structure, and sets of expectations for human action.

Let us take our conflict tools out for a minute. Who benefits from this structural change? Well, we know we must deal with the structure, but who controls the structure? The ordered, routine way that we do things builds in inconsistencies in power, that is, how much control one person or group has over its destiny and choices. Elements of the system are constructed to keep operation of the system "just the way it's always been," which, loosely translated, means that "someone is getting exploited."

With all of our theoretical tools on the table, we can finally launch into an example. Let us take a central human social need: caring for children. The socialization of children has long been a need in human societies. The way a society does this is important, not only because of the type of people with whom we end up in a society, but also because of the effective transfer of culture across generations. This becomes an applied problem when a sociologist is asked to get involved in constructing a system for socialization of the young. Traditionally, and certainly over the past 200 years in the United States, child care has been largely a family affair. Social structure, roles, norms, and even the function of the family itself were geared for socialization. Extended family systems met these needs with cross-generational systems, that is, more than one generation living in the same area or even in the same household. Of course, this type of structure not only cares for the young but is arranged to care for the aging and the old as well. It is a structure, a set of rules for living that works well when people do not need to move around very much. Farming and agricultural lifestyles lend themselves to this fixed-location living.

Of course, over the past two centuries, some demographic and technological factors have had an impact. Infant mortality rates were high, and life expectancy was relatively short. This, coupled with the need for laborers to work in an agricultural technology, produced a constellation of needs that set the stage for an extended family structure: two or more nuclear (mom, dad, and the kids) families living together in proximity. Family roles reflected this need: Mothers provided child care and cognitive and socioemotional maintenance, and fathers were engaged in roles that were external to this role, instrumental in the field and later in the community. The transition that followed throughout industrial and postindustrial societies leads us to the present. How do we structure child care now?

⚜ Research Tools

You probably saw it coming! We are not content to just talk about social structure—we want you to work with it! An effective applied sociologist should be able to build or engineer a social structure. You know that you literally can make a structure into a social thing. It sounds like art, and to some degree, it is. But let us look at a step-by-step process. In this case, we will apply the role of a sociologist as a strategic planner to a problem determining the structure of child care.

Strategic planning is a great example of how to use a variety of basic sociological skills. First, let us define a plan. Barry (1986) defines a plan as "the process of determining what [something] intends to be in the future and how it will get there" (p. 10). Here, we are constructing an organized, formed thing to perform the function of getting from some place in social space and time to a future condition in place and time. You will be laying the superstructure for people to follow. In our example, you would be recommending a routine way that children would be cared for such that the outcome would be an effective system. This is an awesome responsibility and no small task. But as an applied sociologist, you already have many of the tools you need to create a plan.

Let us take planning from the top. First, we need to determine just what we are planning for. We already know that we want to create a system for caring for children. It is a start, but we can move forward from there. If we use our theoretical tools, we will get a jump on the process. From a structural functionalist view, we will do two things. Taking the social system in which our plan will exist as a whole, we need to look around us and determine just what is going on in the social environment. We will do an environmental scan. By doing this, we will take a reading of the social factors that surround us and determine just how they relate to the plan we are about to write. Included in this scan will be direct and indirect assessments of the current status of social institutions and demographic factors. Because we are dealing with child care, we need to assess the child care capability in the existing social system. As a secondary approach, we will need to look at each of the other institutions: economics, government, other family forces, religion, and education. Next, we will also need to track down the demographics: the number of children in each age group and the fertility rates by social grouping.

From here, we need to do a second thing: determine need. Is there a need for the structure we are about to plan? This is critical. Structures will fail to work if they do not serve or fulfill a need. A need is a "discrepancy between a present state (what is) and a desired end state, future state. . . . It is the gap between them" (Witkin & Altschuld, 1995, p. 9). In terms of structure, a need reflects a shortfall between what an existing social structure provides and what it practically or ideally should provide. We rarely expect any social system to run at peak performance or equilibrium where structures and need are in a one-to-one match, but we need to figure how much of a discrepancy exists before we launch into planning.

The place of imagination in all of this is obvious. We may have all of the tools, all of the skills, and perhaps a large share of the necessary knowledge. But unless we are capable of thinking creatively, often to the point of creating worlds that never before existed, the tools will do us little good. It should not surprise anyone that a *vision* is necessary to direct just where it is we are planning to go. Maybe a better way to look at this is through the process we use to create a vision. "Envisioning is a process by which individuals or groups develop a vision or dream of a future state for themselves or their organizations that is . . . clear and powerful to sustain . . . action" (Goodstein, Nolan, & Pfeiffer, 1993, p. 38). This requires communication skill on your part. You need to develop a process by which you can derive this outcome, this vision. One of the exercises in this book will give you the tools to build a vision in a group, but you may rely on a variety of tools that include brainstorming to delphi techniques.

You may run into resistance when you mention creating a vision. There will be many people who will accuse you of being in "la-la land" or Disney World! Get ready, because you will be reminded that the "future is based on the past," and that no one can predict the future. Or people will say, "Even if we get a vision, it will just change!" We have heard this so many times that it makes our heads hurt thinking about it! Do not give up on the vision, because the problem is clear: If we do not have any idea of where we are going, we will never get there! A vision is a magnet that draws us to the future. It does change, it is not static, and, in fact, it may need to be adjusted from time to time. As a sociologist, you know that human interaction is positioned in time and space. The time dimension is comprehensive. It is not just the past, nor is it just the future. It is not even the present *only*. Rather, human interaction is couched in the past, present, and future. We may act in the present, but we need to look both backward and forward. In terms of our example of developing a structure in which we can adequately care for children, we might envision the following: *a vision that may include happy kids who are learning and are free of anxiety and fear; well-fed kids who feel loved and appreciated with high self-esteem and who are surrounded by competent, caring, and consistent adults.* Well, it is a start, and it needs to be honed, tailored a bit by interaction in the group that is creating it. This should become a collective picture in the mind's eye of those creating it.

Now we are ready to focus our structure-creating operation a bit. We need to begin to get more specific: Just what is our purpose for creating this structure? What is our mission? Here, we need to return to our needs assessment, take a look at the gaps between current structure and perceived need, and then factor in our vision. This is an important task, because the vision must reflect reality. Your group then needs to collectively state the purpose of the structure for which we are planning by means of a mission statement. Clear statements of purpose define more directly our planned actions.

This is the point at which planning uses the tools we all have in sociology: the scientific method! We all received basic training in the process of stating a problem, constructing a research design, collecting data, analyzing what we had found, and then stating conclusions. Planning is not wildly different! Mission statements are statements of purpose that reflect the needs, that is, the problems we have uncovered. Our next step is to create a research design. This is the development of the actual structure itself. We need a blueprint for the structure we intend to build. We need to construct some goals and objectives. Rossi and Freeman (1989) define a goal as "a statement, usually general and abstract, of a desired state" (p. 114), whereas they describe objectives as "specific, [concrete] operationalized statements detailing the desired accomplishments of a program" (p. 114). This really works! Why? Because you have been trained to think this way. Defining goals and then creating objectives is not far from defining a concept, reducing it to its identifiable parts, and then measuring the parts. When we do research, we often transform concepts into variables. Following this, we measure the variables through operational definitions. The process in planning is similar, so you have had more practice at it than you probably thought you had.

Mission, goals, objectives, and operational definitions are simply successive levels of concreteness. A mission is abstract. It gets broken into some more manageable parts that are made up of a variety of other parts. In general, it is a reductionist's model (something reduced to its parts); the parts will add up to the whole. As applied sociologists, we need to know that any model will have some shortcomings, and that we will need to fill in the blanks with some other tools. A little qualitative "plaster" would probably help. We are creating structure where there was none. Hence, every plan will have a conceptual part and an operational part. Let us take a look at this.

The vision, mission, and goals will be successively more specific sets of ideas. They are dynamic (i.e., they change), so planning is an ongoing, undulating series of events. You must resist the notion that a plan is rigid. To be effective, planning needs to be ongoing and dynamic. In this sense, there is a "culture-society"-type interaction. The planning concepts form the cultural pieces—the "perceived way we should go" or the "way we should act." This is followed by a structure for action, more of a societal way of handling the plan. The plan makes the transition from idea to action through the planning objectives. That is why objectives need to be measurable. They need to be expressed in terms of actions that can be appraised as to their completeness and depth. The plan's ideas link to the action through the objectives. This is important because when we plan, we are addressing at least three things: knowledge, action, and feelings. Remember that if a plan is effective, it will end up changing the way people know, behave, and feel about the situation in which they find themselves. We would never contend that all of these are successfully delivered, but we need to take them all into account when addressing a plan. Thus, writing a measurable objective is extremely important. So, let us clarify some guidelines for handling them. In this case, we will borrow from Kirschner and Associates (see Rossi & Freeman, 1993). An objective should have the following characteristics:

- *Action or direction of action.* It should use strong verbs. A strong verb is an action-oriented verb that describes an observable or measurable behavior. We often state objectives as infinitives: "to increase," "to decrease"; less strong, but possible: "to improve."
- *What?* An objective should state only one purpose or aim. What do you plan to do?

- *Outcome?* A single end product or result should be included. Clearly state the expected change, effect, success, or outcome that you expect to get. The more precise you are, the better.
- *When?* Finally, indicate the specific time for achievement. When should this action occur?

If you summarize a good objective, it should connect planning concepts to action by stating *WOW*: What action and what Outcome (and what will be the direction of that outcome) will occur by When? Using our child care example (and assuming that a mission and set of goals are in place), we might say that one of our objectives is the following:

> To increase the number of hours of a child's contact with an adult trained in child care by the end of the first quarter of 1998.

What action and what Outcome (and what will be the direction of that outcome):

> To increase the number of hours of a child's contact with an adult trained in child care.

Will occur by When?

By the end of the first quarter of 1998.

There need to be linkages at two ends. The objective must be linked to a goal on one end (which, of course, may be linked to a mission and then to a vision). On the other end, the objective must be tied to a measurement. In our example, the objective must be related to a goal, something like, "to enrich the child-adult relationship environment." Notice that a goal may be a little "gooey"! It is more abstract. On the other end, we will need to count the number of hours of contact and measure the credentials of the adult providing contact. This objective suggests measurements over time, so we will need to measure at least quarterly, but we would probably be better off measuring more frequently, say, daily, and then roll up these measurements into weekly, monthly, and quarterly statistics. In this way, an objective provides a bridge between idea and action/measurement.

It is important to note here the relationship between this thinking and *quality improvement.* Many organizations are designing their plans to use this bridge between concept and outcome to enhance the quality of their social structure. Whether it is called "total quality management" or "continuous improvement" or a variety of other names, the measurability of objectives is extremely important. We create a plan (*plan*); we enact the plan (we *do* it); we *check* it (this is an evaluation step); and then we make changes by *act*ing on the plan (Hunt, 1992). Notice the interplay between ideas, the measurability of objectives in the implementation and checking phase, and the restructuring of the plan in the Act phase. If you write a good set of measurable objectives, evaluating them and checking them for quality will be accomplished more readily.

All along, we have been creating and measuring structure. We need to point out that all structures need not be built from scratch. You will find some prefabricated buildings available in which the blueprints are in existence, so some structures may already have templates. Let us look at some commonly designed structures. In addition to plans, there are at least two other forms of structure that you are likely to encounter: programs and projects. We will be the first to admit that professionals often use these interchangeably, but because you are bound to encounter these sooner or later, let us discuss them. First, definitions. A program is "[an] effort that marshals staff and projects toward some . . . defined . . . goals" (Scriven, 1991, p. 285). Similarly, a project is a set of "time-bounded efforts within a program" (Scriven, 1991, p. 286). Once again, this is pretty direct and follows the same principles we have discussed in the planning procedures outlined previously: A program roughly equals the sum of its projects. Programs and projects are expressed in the form of goals and measurable objectives. A plan is the general structural frame of reference and may embody several programs and even more projects.

This is highly creative and productive work! Knowing which structures to create, when and how, takes us back to our systems tools once again. These ideas fit or nest within one another and hence are interdependent. Plans provide a blueprint for programs, and programs provide the context for projects. As an applied sociologist, you may find yourself building any of these structures. Furthermore, as we demonstrated in our brief discussion of quality improvement, you may also find yourself evaluating these structures. Regardless, we hope you will readily see the connections between our field of study and some very practical skills.

§ Presentation Tools

The concept of structure is elusive. It is difficult to envision. Therefore, presenting information on structure requires a technique that will allow your audience to truly "see it with pictures." You might want to "say it with pictures"! Any mechanism for converting these abstractions into a more concrete form is important. Here are some ideas that may help you to enlighten your clients while increasing both their understanding and involvement.

Sketching a Structure

You need to see what you are thinking and talking about. You will need at least two pictures: the structure as it is, and the structure as you want it to be. Freehand drawing for this purpose is a great first step. Honestly, some great ideas started out on the back of a paper napkin! Over coffee or lunch, some ideas start to flow, and before you know it, someone has a pen out and is scrawling a diagram. You may soon find that others are converting their thoughts to pictures; finally, you have a great graphic presentation of the structure you are describing. The idea then becomes "something." The value, of course, is that now you can manipulate the "things," move them around, and write on them. After all, we have made a case for treating structure as a thing.

Of course, you are not restricted to napkins for your diagrams! You might want to carry some 3×5 cards in your pocket at all times just for this purpose (and other forms of brainstorming as well). A pen or pencil and paper are powerful tools for this type of work. You might want to buy a plastic template (the kind used for flowcharting can be useful here) to help you convert your ideas to "prettier" diagrams. Computer software for drawing organization charts is plentiful, and this can be valuable both for the earlier conceptualization of structure and for the formal report that you will present to your client.

Now research the structure as it is. This will require interviewing the clients in the work environment, reviewing existing organizational structures, and understanding from key informants (those people who are most likely to know) just what they interpret the structure to be. Here, sociology is once again valuable. Remember that there will likely be a formal and an informal structure for conducting business. The formal structure exists "on paper" as part of formal organizational policy. The informal structure is the one that people really use to get work done. So, it is likely that you will end up with two or more diagrams of how things work.

Comparing the Pictures

Now that you have drawn the formal and informal diagrams of the structure, you can construct a structural alternative. This picture is the result of at least three factors:

1. The discrepancy between the formal and informal pictures that you have already drawn
2. The input from clients and key informants about how the structure should look
3. Creative professional input from you

The outcome is a proposed structure. It is "proposed" because you will need to make some adjustments based on feedback from the clients. You will need to make a series of presentations. Let us take these in turn.

Presenting the Structures

Now you can engage in an innovative next step that combines brainstorming and your sociological understanding of structure. Your proposed structure is not the end-all but a model for discussion. You will need to get feedback from clients before you ever recommend it. This will be an iterative process. In other words, you will go back and forth between groups of people, key informants, and stakeholders. For each group, you will need input on the perceptions of all of the pictures: formal, informal, and proposed. You are looking for consensus—agreement on what the structure should look like. For this presentation, you will want the pictures to look nicer, that is, cleaned up. Here, some computer-generated graphics would be valuable. These can be presented in several ways.

1. Through electronic presentations using Powerpoint®, CorelDraw®, or a similar graphics package with supporting computer and electronic projection equipment.
2. On transparencies and an overhead projector. These may be in color or black and white. They are portable and easy to do (many transparencies may be made by copying your picture onto the transparency by using a photocopier).
3. On paper. Of course, this can be in color or black and white.

For the preliminary presentations for feedback purposes, you will probably want to keep it simple. Use black-and-white transparencies and copies on paper to discuss the proposed structure. Feedback from these sessions will lead you to a final picture of the structure that is most relevant for the client. When you reach the final presentation, you will want to provide a pictorial presentation that shows the evolution of the structure: from a formal/informal first set to an intermediate design to the final design. Of course, your final presentation should be polished. You may want to provide more color, such as an electronic presentation and color handouts. Of course, black-and-white copies and overhead transparencies will still get the job done effectively.

▧ Sociologist as Expert

Understanding structure is central to sociology. The organizational "reengineering," so common in postindustrial societies, is a perfect target for applying sociology. The downsizing and right-sizing movements ask several clearly sociological questions. We will take these questions in turn, showing the sociologist's place in each.

Let us look at three basic questions that would be relevant to organization redesign:

1. What functions should the organization perform? "What should it do?"
2. How should the organization be structured to perform these functions?
3. What impact will this structure produce?

What functions? Virtually all sociologists are taught to measure and interpret social needs. The structural functionalist tools that we have mentioned in this book are particularly valuable here. Our sociology will help us determine the intended and unintended functions that need to be performed by the organization. Elements of the organization that are dysfunctional or eufunctional may cease to exist. A needs assessment, followed by recommendations for organizational function, is part of an applied sociologist's repertoire.

Let us turn to the second question, "How should the organization be structured?" Architects tell us, "Form (often) follows function." Applied sociologists know this well when it comes to social forms. The internal beliefs, values, and norms of a structure need to be aligned with the functions and, therefore, the needs of the social environment in which it is located. Applied sociologists will be sensitive to look in two other directions from their view in a contemporary needs assessment: the past and the future. An applied sociologist will be particularly sensitive to looking toward the past to uncover the cultural roots of the social organization to be restructured. This is critical in making sure that key formal and informal structures are not removed in error. In addition, an eye toward the future is essential. How viable is this organization likely to be in the future? Other chapters in this book address future issues, including the impact of change, leadership, and the value of studying the future. For now, suffice it to say that a sociologist will need to look at future trends and help gauge the impact of future social forces on this organization.

Finally, what impact will this change in structure have? Again, applying sociology can have immense value. Although we could take many views on this specific situation, let us examine it from the three levels of social organization: meso, macro, and micro. The changes to the organization are being made at the meso (middle) level of social organization. In essence, that is where we are assuming that this organization resides. Clearly, there will be changes at this level, but what will happen above and below the organization? Let us look above, toward the macro level. The sociological perspective makes us aware that we will need to examine the societal level forces that impinge on this organization and the reaction that society will have to the internal structural change. In addition, we will need to continuously update our "environmental scan" of social and demographic trends and the interaction of restructuring with these trends.

Importantly, we must question the impact our restructuring will have on individual employees: the micro level. Sociologists recognize that each social self is embedded in social structure. Changing social structure not only changes the external organization of life, but it also challenges the understanding and definition of the people in the group. Changing the structure changes the definition of self. This varies from the anomie ("normlessness") that occurs when one loses his or her job through downsizing, to the redefinition of self that comes from taking on a new role because of restructuring. Regardless of the level of analysis or the assessment of impact, sociological perspectives and problems of structure are complementary.

ⓜ Case Study

A local high technology company plans to restructure the way its employees work on a daily basis. The chief executive officer (CEO) has decided that all 40 employees in the company will be telecommuting from their homes in the next 5 to 6 weeks. He informs his employees that they will soon be making the change. Reflecting on this decision, he has hired you to evaluate the impact on his employees that this change in the work structure will have. The company's CEO is very sensitive to his employees' needs. He is very concerned that the fit between the new organization of work and his employees' needs is a good one. Naturally, he is concerned that his clients may suffer in this change, so he needs feedback on the impact of this restructuring.

Your task is to evaluate this restructuring project. Sociologists and other professionals are often hired to conduct evaluation research. Evaluation requires the rigorous use of research procedures in applied settings to determine the success of projects, programs, or processes (summative evaluation) and/or to provide recommendations for project, program, or process improvement (formative evaluation; Scriven, 1967). Evaluations may be internal and/or external to the project. In short, we may think of the types of evaluations in this manner:

	Formative	Summative
Internal	a	b
External	c	d

Internal evaluations are performed by people within the project to determine if the project has been successful (b), to make recommendations for project improvement (a), or both (a and b). External evaluations are conducted by people outside the project for similar purposes (project success, d; project improvement, c; or both, c and d). Although you have been hired as an external evaluator, this does not rule out the possibility that the company has already attempted an internal evaluation.

The company has given you a limited budget and has indicated that although you may do some primary data collection (go out in the field and collect some new data), the CEO has asked you to make every effort to use data resources already available in the company. The company has an extensive management information system (MIS). They keep track of (monitor) employee work rates, hours on their computer systems, and other productivity measures. The company is small, and you will find that company leaders are very sensitive to employee needs. How would you handle this project?

Possible Solutions

Here are some ways to think of a solution to this problem. When you engage a client for an evaluation, you need to examine "Five D's" (Steele, 1996). For each evaluation, you need to *define it, design it, decode and encode it, do it,* and *deliver it.* Let us take these in turn.

Define It

You cannot evaluate something unless you know what it is. That sounds simple, but this can be the most difficult part. Earlier in this chapter, we looked at some structures that may be evaluated: plans, programs, processes, and projects, to name a few. First, through a client interview, you need to determine which of the following this case is. In short, you need to check all that apply below:

What are you evaluating?

Plan? A plan is "the process of determining what [something] intends to be in the future and how it will get there" (Barry, 1986, p. 10).

Program? A program is "[an] effort that marshals staff and projects toward some . . . defined . . . goals" (Scriven, 1991, p. 285).

Project? A project is a "time-bounded effort within a program" (Scriven, 1991, p. 286).

Process? A process is "what happens between input and output, between start and finish" in a system (Scriven, 1991, p. 277).

In this case, moving to a telecommuting structure may have multiple definitions. It is at least a project and a process. For both, you need to determine all of the following:

> The mission: What is the purpose?
> The goals: What are the general valued conditions that the client wishes to achieve?
> The objectives: Specifically, what is supposed to happen to achieve the goals?
> What outcomes are expected from the project?

The objectives must be stated as clearly as possible, and they must be measurable. Two important issues emerge here. First, these objectives may be "stated" and "unstated." The stated objectives may be written down in company documents; the unstated objectives may not. Rather, unstated objectives may just be common knowledge—what everybody knows. Both types of objectives are extremely important; that is, one type is as real as the other for creating outcomes.

Second, objectives must be measurable. In short, we must be able to put a number on them (quantitative) or record that they happened (qualitative). If the objectives are not measurable, they didn't happen! The measured outcomes are the project success measures. In an evaluation, these measures are very important.

You no doubt recognize that we have already discussed these items earlier in the chapter. So, a few minutes rereading the discussion of mission, goals, and objectives, as well as understanding their relationship to one another, may be very helpful. Processes have missions, goals, and objectives also, but they are a little different in their nature. (You may need to skip ahead to Chapter 3 to better understand the concept of process.)

Design It

Now you need to determine a strategy for researching this evaluation. *Design it* means that you will create a blueprint for it. The "it" we are addressing here is the procedure for doing the evaluation. This is a point at which you will need to reach into your sociological bag of tools. Select a design that works in this setting and employ it. In general, designs fall into two categories: experimental and quasi-experimental.

Experimental designs are central to science. In short, they are structured as follows:

Before the Introduction of the Project or Treatment	Introduction of the Project or Treatment "X"	After the Introduction of the Project or Treatment
Experimental (or "treatment" group • Measure the outcome measures, success measures, measurable objectives (Y)	Experimental (or "treatment") group *gets the project*, program, or training; in short, "the treatment"	Experimental (or "treatment") group • Measure the outcome measures, success measures, measurable objectives (Y)
The control or comparison group • Measure the outcome measures, success measures, measurable objectives (Y)	The control or comparison group *does not* get the project, program, or training; in short, "the treatment"	The control or comparison group • Measure the outcome measures, success measures, measurable objectives (Y)

Randomly assign cases to one of the three sections: before the project/ treatment, introduction of the project/treatment, or after the project/treatment.

Experimental/Treatment Group
1. Measure the outcome measures, success measures, and measurable objectives in the group that will be involved in the project.
2. Enact the project or treatment for this group.
3. Measure the outcome measures, success measures, and measurable objectives in the group that has been involved in the project.

Control Group (It becomes a comparison group
if people were not randomly assigned to it!)
1. Measure the outcome measures, success measures, and measurable objectives in the group that will *not* be involved in the project.
2. Do not enact the project or treatment for this group.
3. Measure the outcome measures, success measures, and measurable objectives in the group that has not been involved in the project.

Simply stated, quasi-experimental designs are designs that do not conform to this structure. You immediately see that it is rare that you will be able to use an experimental design in an applied setting. Unfortunately, quasi-experimental designs do not have the same strength as their experimental counterparts. Nevertheless, as an applied sociologist, you are challenged to create the most rigorous design that you can for the problem that you have.

One final note: Designs are not techniques. A design is the general plan for doing this evaluation. A technique is a specific procedure for actually gathering the data you need. For example, you may decide to employ a survey or a focus group (or both!) to gather the information needed to evaluate this project. These tools need to be crafted before you leave this step.

Decode and Encode It

This step is really done simultaneously with Defining and Designing. Here, you are making sure that you know what will be measured and how you will measure it. For this case, objectives related to the strengths and weaknesses of the restructuring effort in our case study must be measured. Measurement is critical to all research, and it is really done simultaneously with all of the other steps in the evaluation process. Basically, you are determining just how you will know that the ideas, concepts, even the program or project itself, are really happening. For example, if worker satisfaction was supposed to improve because of a series of team-building workshops, we would need to measure worker satisfaction. We could create a satisfaction instrument employing some satisfaction measures that ask workers to self-report on whether they "strongly agree, agree, are undecided, disagree, or strongly disagree" with a list of job-related statements. We might also consider measuring, or encoding, their satisfaction by reviewing absenteeism: how often they miss work. Notice that both ways attempt to measure something: one way asks people directly; the other makes note of their behavior. In either case, we are attempting to encode what they are doing or saying to determine if our workshops were successful.

Do It

Now that you know what you are evaluating, you have created a design with appropriate techniques for gathering data, and you have determined appropriate measures, you are ready to go into the field and implement your evaluation plan. Be prepared, and be flexible. Collecting data is a time-consuming and dynamic process. By dynamic, we mean that things happen that you might not expect! Respondents refuse to participate, or they get sick. Information you never anticipated emerges—you need to be ready!

Deliver It

When you are delivering an evaluation project to a client, be guided by at least two rules:

1. Write clearly and simply.
2. Construct your report to conform to the client's world—his or her corporate culture. The worst report is one that is not *read and understood* by the audience or audiences for whom it was intended.

This overview simply lays the groundwork for dealing with this case. As we have indicated in this and upcoming chapters, each case reflects *a number of different audiences, and the techniques must be tailored to each of these groups. Above all, remember to be creative and to make it an enjoyable learning exercise.*

ᛜ Exercises

Here are a few exercises that will help you identify structure and the impact of change within structure. These exercises require a combination of life experiences and your understanding of structure.

1. Pick a social situation at the micro (self or person) level, the meso (the group/organizational) level, and the macro (societal) level. Identify the social situation at each level. Describe the situation; that is, indicate what is going on. For each situation, describe its structure. In other words, describe the nature of this socially constructed, organized social form that guides human action.

2. Select a structure in which you currently participate. This could be an interpersonal relationship, a group, an organization, or another structure. From your position on the inside of this structure, indicate the set of norms, values, and beliefs that seem to guide human action. What passes for common knowledge? In other words, what is viewed as common sense? Does the structure have any impact on the culture, the way of life going on around you?

3. Locate two groups that, in essence, do the same thing, such as two supermarkets, two families, two restaurants, two churches . . . it is

your choice. Visit each of these groups. Describe the structure for each. Now compare them. How are the structures different? How are they similar? Explain why they are similar and why they are different.

4. Watch the television news or read the newspaper at the local, regional, or national/international level. List the organizations that in some way have reported a change in structure in the past week. For each structure, indicate the level of organization and which aspects of the structure have changed. Then, assess the impact that this change may have had on the people inside and outside of the structure.

5. Select any group or organization. Produce a plan for reengineering it. Diagram the new structure. Outline the differences between the old structure and the new one. What will be the differences in the input, output, and internal processes? What impact would your change have on the people in the structure and on the functions that the structure performs?

When Process Is the Problem

Like structure, sociologists could easily spend much of their professional lives dealing with process. Again, this makes sense. Sociology is the study of human interaction, and process is an example of organized interaction. Applied sociologists can add value to the understanding and solving of problems related to process. The quality improvement movement in business, health care, education, and government has emphasized the need to understand process. Let us see how this works.

In many ways, we will use the concepts from the previous chapter to begin our explanation of process. That is because one of the characteristics of process is its structure. Scriven (1991) identifies process as "what happens between input and output, between start and finish" in a system (p. 277). This is a good start and a reasonable approach. But what are these "things"? One reasonable response is that they are structures. They are organized systems of interactions that get us from input to output. Hence, they are guided by norms or rules for action.

◊ What Is Process?

Applied social scientists are often tempted to ignore process. From this view, process is a "black box." In other words, people go into the process, this black box, they act—bounce around inside for a while—and then they come out changed. Often, the focus is on the outcome. What happened as a result of the black box? In an assessment of process, we get inside the black box and determine how it works. The basic assumption is that the structure of the process will have something to do with the outcome. Here is an example.

Compare a baseball game with a boxing match. Although they may seem wildly different on the surface, their processes have much in common. First, the nature of the process is competition. By definition, competition as a process has several characteristics. In competition, there are rules for how the game is played and rules for who will be declared a winner and who will become a loser. Fighting is not permitted in the baseball process (once in a while, it happens); batting is not allowed in a boxing match! In both cases, process is monitored and regulated by those who have the duty of maintaining the rules: umpires and referees. Norms are everywhere: the weight and size of the ball, the weight and size of the boxing gloves, the weight of the fighters, the number of players. The list seems endless. Sanctions are placed on failure to comply.

In both cases, two competitors or two teams enter the stadium or the ring (input) at an appointed time and space. They work through a system of patterned interactions that is somewhat linear: it starts at Time A and moves ahead to Time B. After the application of the baseball or boxing processes, someone is declared a winner (output) through a structured process of assigning points. We could chart the flow of people through the baseball process and the procedures and decisions made that result in a decision and then an end in the process. Those who excel in either of these sports probably have personal and social factors that suit them to the process. How does this example translate into applied sociology?

Recently, improving quality of products and services has shifted the focus from the individual worker to the process of how work is done. Sociologists have had this approach for many years, but we are rarely identified as professionals who see the world this way. Let us try to make sense of process. We need to assess all of the components, all of the things that could be part of a process: all of the things between input and output. Of course, there are people in the system, and truly, their personalities do count. But as applied sociologists, our contribution is most likely to be tied to the sociological things that we find end to end in a social system. Now, let us go back to one of our theoretical tools, namely, structural functionalism and its systems approach to social action. A process is a definable human situation. It has two major sets of parts: substance and action. In short, process is both static and dynamic. It is something (substance), but it is changing all the time (action). Process is structured, it is ordered, it has shape, and it becomes thinglike (i.e., it is reified). Hence, process has all of the components of structure. Because it is thinglike, we can address it as such and work on it. At the same time, because it is a human construction, we can build it. We can make it whatever we want it to be.

Because process is structured, it is made up of the basic building blocks of structure: norms. Now, let us look at the other side of process: action and, perhaps more importantly, interaction. Using the structural functionalist tools, we rarely find a social unit that does not have a function. A process exists as an interconnected set of actions that have been constructed to get something done. So, the norms are connected in such a way as to guide action and produce an outcome. In a process, humans interact in predictable ways. Often, they fulfill roles and statuses. The process becomes a system: a whole unit with interactive parts that has meaning within a culture. It becomes a way to do something.

Extending the functionalist idea, these processes may become dysfunctional. This system of organized parts simply may not perform the function it was meant to accomplish. The reason for this may be internal and/or external. Internally, the norms and roles that are central may not be dynamic enough to keep up with the external changes that have surrounded it. The organizational reengineering activity of the 1990s is an example of this response. Downsizing and right-sizing were buzzwords that related to the change in process. In downsizing, layers of organization, related roles, and, of course, people in those roles are eliminated to make an organization more efficient. It is hoped that in the process of eliminating structure, the reorganization of the social system was "right"—able to meet the needs of the organization effectively.

Once again, basic sociological tools are useful in applied settings dealing with process. Reflecting on Merton's (1968) classic work, we remember the value of conceptualizing human social life as a contrast between cultural goals and institutional means (this is usually cited in relationship to deviance, but here we will take another approach). A process likely emerges because a group, a culture, or a corporation responds to a need. You will recall that this need may be tied to a vision, the vision to a mission, and the mission to a set of goals. These abstract statements of value—this place where the group wants to be—sets up a condition in which one must answer the question, "How do we get there?" The set of steps taken to get to the end result Merton saw as institutional means. We might view this "means to an end" as a process. So, a process turns out to be a lattice of norms structured between the input and the output.

Now, this meaning may transcend a corporate culture, or it may be central to it. The notion of culture as "a way of life" is critical here (Schein, 1992). Culture and corporate culture, for example, are ways of doing things. As an applied sociologist, you will need to listen to people when they say, "We don't do things that way around here." They are often talking about engaging in normative process behavior. Hence, process becomes a way to direct how things are done as well as what is done. How people conduct their daily work is in large part supported by the corporate way of life. The processes become embedded in the culture, and they are difficult to change. Very often, just getting people to "think outside the box" is a valuable ingredient in changing process.

So, a process turns out to be a means to an end and an end in itself. Processes start to become forces in their own right. Because they are structures, we treat them like things. Here is what we mean. The flow of paperwork through a company, of people through a mass transportation system, or of patients through a health clinic are all examples of structured processes. People, information, or products move through this system of normed interactions to some outcome. At each point in the process, some change takes place. If we look at the process as made up only of people, we may make some serious mistakes. How human action occurs in this structure is largely based on the norms within.

As applied sociologists, we may be called upon to work on a process in at least one of two ways. We may be asked to address an existing process, or we may be asked to create a new process. Let us look at each of these. There are similarities and differences in changing existing processes and creating new ones. In either case, we need to check our sociological toolbox for clues as to how we might approach our task. Let us take this process, step by step.

◪ Research Tools

Because process is structured, we will want you to work on it! Applied sociologists can do their part to engineer or reengineer a social process. Once again, we will make this social reality thinglike so that we can work with it more easily. Recall our discussion of strategic planning in the previous chapter. We will need to remember the planning procedure and the elements of a plan (vision, mission, goals, objectives, actions) in order to effectively act on a process. We will look at two actions we can take: (a) changing an existing process and (b) creating a new process.

Whether working with a process that is in place or starting from scratch to build something new, we are faced with an initial concern: What process is needed here? The answer to this question lies at the end of a formal or informal needs assessment. By using survey research, focus groups, and key informant interviews, you can identify the key functions that this process is expected to perform. In discovering them, we have defined the purpose of the process and hence have addressed two elements in the planning process: the vision for the process and its mission.

If the process is in place, once we are armed with a mission, we can continue, step by step, to determine just what is going on and, if appropriate, to recommend an alternative process. Hence, our next step is to describe the process. Our task is to answer the question, "What is going on here?" You may need to do some exploratory research here. You will need to investigate what people are doing and how they are doing it. Do not be surprised if people in the process have very little knowledge or understanding of just what is going on beyond their own place in the system. You might expect something like this to occur in large, hierarchical, segmented organizations.

This type of organization has the work it does broken down into pieces. A procedure is broken into segments, and each segment is completed separately from the whole. Eventually, the segments are assembled into the whole, and something is produced. This system is characterized by top-down management with extensive and multiple levels of statuses. You should not be surprised if people who occupy a role in this pyramid have little sense of the whole. This is only one structure for a process; there are many other, perhaps even infinite combinations for processes. The key here is that you need to determine the characteristics of the process before any meaningful change can occur.

To do this, you need to take a look at the process. We recommend that you draw a picture of it. Plain and simple, a picture will help you understand several things: the structure of the process, the completeness of the system (are there any loose ends or process paths that go nowhere?), and the properties (qualities) of the process. How can we do this? Fortunately, we can construct a flowchart to determine this. Flowcharts are commonly used in many fields, not the least of which are the computer systems professions. The good news is that there are a variety of uniform symbols that make it possible to understand flow through a

- Start (and Stop)

- Process (Doing something)

- Decision (Yes? No?)

- Stop (Start)

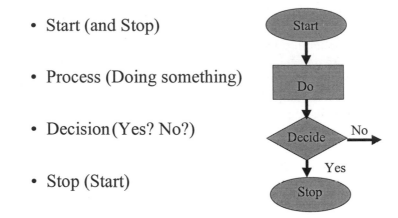

Figure 3.1 Basic Flowchart Symbols

system. The bad news is that there are a large number of these symbols. But you can do most flowcharting by using three basic symbols (see Figure 3.1). These three are ovals (to designate the beginning and the end of the process: "Start" and "Stop"); rectangles (to designate processing—doing something to the object of the process); and diamonds (to designate decisions: "If Yes," go this way, "If No," go this way). Notice that the pictured process has a downward movement until a decision is reached. This particular process really does not use decisions effectively. If we decide "yes," we end the process. If we decide "no," we end up nowhere! Let us develop this process a little more with an example. Suppose we are screening applicants for a job. We decide that in the first phase of the hiring process, we want to receive applications (start→process). Our next step is to decide whether we want to accept a person. If we accept him or her, we want him or her to move to a training program. If we reject a person, we want to notify him or her professionally of our decision and remove him or her from the pool of applicants. What would this process look like?

The next step is to measure the flow through the process. To do this, you will need to determine the roles in the system—just who does what? At what point do we find this behavior in the system? Then, we need to determine the nature of the units flowing through the system. What is supposed to happen? There is a velocity to a process. We need to determine how quickly something effectively moves through the system. Of course, there are other concerns. Clients will be interested in the cost of performing the process and the benefits received. Products, forms, and people move through the process at a rate of speed that is the number of products divided by units of time. A process has an efficiency level based on its capacity to do what it is "supposed" to do. We need to be able to determine just what is happening at each step in the process. Is there a log jam anywhere? Is the work backing up at some critical point? Additionally, we need to determine the expense incurred in these log jams. Processes need to be effective (do what they are supposed to do) and cost-effective (minimize unnecessary costs in conducting the process). Remember, there will likely be both formal and informal versions of the process. If the process described formally on paper does not work for employees, they may create their own version that seems more effective to them. The fact is, they may be correct, or they may not! In either case, your analysis should indicate objectively what and how the process is transpiring.

Next, revisit the process mission. When your goal is to restructure a process, then you need to find out just what the process is intended to do. This means a return to the mission and the goals for this process. This may be yet another challenge. Michael Patton, a prominent evaluator, might label this as a "goal-free" situation (Patton, 1990). People may be involved in a process but be unable to tell you just what it is supposed to do. They may not be able to determine the overall goals or the purpose for doing what they are doing.

Let us turn to a little basic sociology. Once again, we may apply the concepts to the process as a problem. A process, like any structure, is made up of norms. Norms are tied to collective values, and values are related to beliefs. All of this is anchored in the mission and vision for the organization. If the elements of planning discussed in the previous chapter are a little unclear, go back and review them. The shape of the process should reflect the mission of the organization, or at least the mission of the unit in the organization that you are analyzing. If what people are doing is not aligned with what the process is intended to do, then we have a discrepancy, a problem. You may need to run some focus groups or key informant interviews to get this exploratory information.

Suppose that no process exists. The initial procedure for constructing a new process is similar to what we have already discussed. Once again, consider using a needs assessment. Not surprisingly, establishing a purpose for the process is again important. Here is the point at which sociologists can excel. Sociologists know that the shortest distance between two points is not always a straight line! A way of getting the job done may be discontinuous in the corporate culture. For organizational or technological reasons, the most direct procedure simply may not work. For example, eliminating or changing someone's work role may make perfect sense on paper. But if the labor unions in the organization or senior management do not agree with your proposal, you may quickly find that your proposed process will not work. The value of the conflict perspective and the notion of cultural relativity have special meaning at this point. Your process may appear to be aerodynamically sound, but will it fly? Let us consider why you may never get off the ground!

Your new process will be a synthesis. Remember, you are trying to get people to do things they have not done quite this way before. This is social change, and it does not come easily. You must be culturally sensitive to the way of life in the organization and the power centers inside and outside. To what extent can your process be implemented if key people do not understand and/or support it? If the common sense of the organization is inconsistent with the proposed process, the likelihood of success is diminished. We encourage you to consider the introduction of a new process as an ongoing process in which you obtain client buy-in along the way. The next section demonstrates some ways that you can include your clients in reengineering. Effectively integrating client input into the process and communicating your model for your client's process are both essential.

〽 Presentation Tools

Process is often difficult for people to imagine. Like many social forms, participants may not envision that they are part of something bigger than themselves. So, your presentation on process requires visual images. As we recommended in the chapter on structure, your audience will benefit if they can "see it with pictures." Here are two ways to present this information: one way is static, and the other is dynamic. The first just helps you to create and to tell the story. The second encourages your audience to get involved in it.

Diagram the Process

In this chapter, we have discussed the value of a flowchart. A picture of your chart is essential when it is time for your presentation. The number of diagrams of this chart is a function of the descriptions and comparisons that you plan to make. For example, if you plan to compare the current process with a new one, you will need at least two pictures: (a) the current process and (b) the process as you expect it to be. Plastic templates are available if you want to sketch these by hand. Check the computer science or management information systems part of a college bookstore. You may even find these where you buy your computer hardware and software.

If you are using key informant interviews or focus groups to get information, the template, a pencil, and a scratch pad are great tools. Remember, this stage is the beginning of an iterative process. That is, you will do it over and over again. Make sure you have a big eraser! You do not always need a computer. Getting a working sketch of the flowchart for a process is a good start. You will find that although people are engaged in the process every day, they may not have consensus on just how it works. Chances are good that few people, if any, have seen the entire process. Keep translating thoughts into pictures until you have a comprehensive graphic presentation of the process you are describing. When your audience can see the process, they will begin to understand it more clearly.

Let us consider for a moment the sequence of events that has occurred thus far. First, you work with a group of clients to sketch a flowchart that depicts the process as it is now. Remember that there will likely be a formal and an informal process. You may find multiple shared realities, hence, more than two flowcharts. Second, from focus groups, survey data, and observation, you sketch an alternative process. This is the process as it might be. You clean up these drawings, and you write a description for each explaining the process in words. For now, this might be just an outline.

Comparing the Pictures

Now compare the processes. Like our discussion of structure in Chapter 2, the process analysis will be an assessment of the following:

1. The discrepancy between the formal and informal pictures that you have already drawn
2. The input from clients and key informants about how the structure should look
3. Creative professional input from you

The outcome is a "proposed" process. You will still need feedback from clients.

Presenting the Structures

Your paper-and-pencil drawings may be adequate for intermediate presentations and discussion, but you will probably want something more formal when you make your presentation to the stakeholders in the project. Once you are sure that the flowcharts are ready, turn to a computer software package that will help you make the presentation suitable for presentation. We do not advocate any particular brand of software, but a package such as Visio Express can be helpful here. Create your flow diagrams on electronic or hard copy, and then prepare them for presentation with software such as PowerPoint or Corel presentation packages. Put them on disk or on transparency for use in your presentation. "Bulleted" outlines discussing the flow through the process should accompany these pictures. By bulleted, we mean that the outline should provide key points only. For example:

- The process starts,
- It enters procedure one,
- A decision is made to . . . ,
- The process stops.

No matter what we learned in college, we have found that keeping it simple is very important. You may want to provide photocopies for your audience as well.

Feedback from these sessions may lead to a final picture for the process. Depending on the outcome of the presentation, at least four things can happen: (a) the client will accept your work without revision, (b) he or she will accept it with revision, (c) the client will reject it but request revision, or (d) the client will reject it and not ask for revision. In the first three alternatives, you are still in the game. You probably want to avoid the fourth alternative! If you land in the second or third alternative, you will find yourself back in the data collection, flow-diagram-drawing business again. Collect more data, and continue the process of defining the process until you have agreement or until the contract runs out!

Here is another way to handle the creation of a new process design. This procedure gets the clients involved in some hands-on brainstorming.

1. Draw three flow diagram symbols on paper: (a) the oval for start and stop, (b) the diamonds for decision making, and (c) the rectangle for processing. You may use your plastic template for this, or you may use a computer package. Make the symbols big enough so that you can put a small Post-it® note on each, but small enough that you can put several of them on a tabletop.
2. Now, label each picture accordingly; one picture for each of the following: (a) start, stop; (b) decision; and (c) processing.
3. Put the symbols on a photocopier and make multiple copies. You will need more rectangles and triangles than ovals! Make the copies on cover stock (some thicker paper that will help here).
4. Cut out the symbols.
5. Now, get some Post-it® notes or a similar type of stick-on note and several pencils.
6. Gather the key clients who will be involved in the process design. You may wish to break the group into several teams.
7. Explain the meaning of each of the flowchart symbols.
8. Allowing an hour or more, give each client or each client team a pack of symbols. On a flat, dry surface (like a tabletop), engage the clients in a brainstorming session in which they physically create the flowchart by arranging the symbols in the shape of their perception of the process's configuration.
9. Encourage debate, dialogue, and discussion. Use the Post-it® notes to explain the action that is taking place at each decision or process.
10. Stop the action and ask the participants to walk around to each version of the flowchart. Of course, if there is only one flowchart, you may stop.
11. Discuss the process. How do the participants perceive it? What are its strengths and weaknesses? Why did they construct it this way?
12. Record the diagram and the rationale.

Now you have accomplished three important things. First, you have a flow diagram created by the people who need to understand and use it. Second, you have consensus on the shape of the process. Finally, your clients have been engaged in the procedure, and in this sense, they own it.

⚍ Sociologist as Expert

Are sociologists uniquely qualified to do process reengineering? If this means that sociologists are the only ones who can do it, the

answer to this question would be "No!" The bigger question is, Why
have applied sociologists not taken on restructuring? Once again, applied sociology would be an excellent fit for this type of work. The systems view of sociology and the holistic view of a problem would contribute to the understanding of the dimensions of a process.
Furthermore, sociologists would immediately understand that nature
of a process as embedded in other social systems. Finally, sociologists doing applied work would be unlikely to overlook the intended
and unintended consequences of changing a process. Let us take these
in turn.

The functionalist perspective in sociology encourages us to view
a process as a system. We can return to the three questions we asked of
structure in the previous chapter, but in this case, we can apply the
questions to process:

1. What functions should the process perform? What should it do?
2. How should the process be structured to perform these functions?
3. What impact will this process produce?

What functions? This is really an application of the planning process. What is the mission—the purpose—of this process? This question
is valuable whether we plan to create a new process or assess an old
one. The question of purpose is central to reasoned structures, things
that humans have collectively created. We may need to step back again
and reflect on the social need that is present. Creating a clear picture of
purpose and need grounds the process in substance. Sociologists
would be valuable in conducting needs assessments to map the elements of the process that would be necessary to get the job done. They
could help with the roles and role definitions as well as the organizational units that could be assembled to cover intended functions within
the process.

Sociology can provide special help in structuring the process.
When evaluating a current process for restructuring, sociology's repertoire of skills and perspectives would once again be valuable. Sociologists add value to this project by mapping the unintended, latent
functions that have currently evolved in the old process. Finding elements of the process that are dysfunctional or without function is also
a significant application of skills. A process evaluation that serves as a
barometer of the process's impact (summative) and that provides rec-

ommendations for change (formative) are both likely tools in a process redesign problem.

Assessing the impact of a changing structure adds immense value. Here, we see the comparable problems we faced in our general discussion of structure in the previous chapter. From a sociological view, the process is likely to be embedded in larger social systems. This forces us to look up and down as well as side to side. Looking up, we will want to know if this process is intrinsically tied into some other system at a level of social organization above it. We need to determine the linkage of the meso to the macro, for example. Similarly, we need to look down. Are there processes below this one that are dependent on it? Here, we may be viewing the connection of microlevel processes to mesolevel. Clearly, we need to determine processes that are networked at the same level. If we are assessing a process and its impact, the impact may resonate in all directions. Taking this 360-degree look around a process is valuable and reflective of a sociologic view. Because need may arise in all directions, impact may be felt in all directions. One must systematically assess the intended and likely unintended outcomes of a change in process. Remember, humans (as well as other resources) are personally and functionally embedded in this structure. Any adjustment to it will be felt at varying levels throughout.

▨ Case Study

Again, the importance of understanding process as the problem is a critical element in quality improvement. Total quality management or continuous improvement models rely on process analysis or reengineering to improve how they conduct business. Suppose a local company complains of having trouble hiring and keeping good people. You meet with the chief executive officer, who shows you salary studies that indicate that his company pays comparable salary and benefits with others in the area. He wonders if there is something wrong with the people he's hiring.

Many things could be problematic here. But this time, your task is to look at the hiring process. You set out to conduct a process evaluation. We can return to the Five D's that we discussed in the previous chapter for an outline.

Define It

In this case, we are working on a process. We need to determine several things about the process:

1. What are the boundaries of the process? Here, we want to know where the process starts and stops.
2. What does the process look like? Draw a flowchart of the process. Determine the roles and role expectations for people and groups in the process.
3. What is it supposed to do? Determine the mission, goals, objectives, and outcomes that are expected from the process.

Design It

Now you must decide how you will research the process.

1. What function(s) is the process intended to fulfill? This may sound a little redundant from Item 3 above. The difference is that in this stage, we might want to do some primary research. A needs assessment and some exploratory research will help us determine the answers to this question. This question is critical because it sets baselines, or fundamental definitions and guidelines for comparison.
2. You may be able to create a quasi-experimental design. From your diagram of the flowchart in the definition phase and your needs assessment, you may move toward a strategy in which you can compare three conditions: (a) what the process is, (b) what it currently is expected to be, and (c) what it could be. This design means that you will need researched models for each.
3. Techniques employed here could vary. Surveys among workers, managers, and those who have participated in the hiring process would help gauge present and ideal states for the process. Focus groups would provide some "what" and "how" types of data for process design. Secondary analysis of company records would likewise provide valuable information on the flow through the process.

Decode and Encode It

In this step, you are making sure that you know what will be measured and how you will measure it. As a start, you will likely need to do the following:

1. Determine the success measures that the stakeholders indicate to be important to the process. The clients may know best what they need from

the system, and they can tell you the indicators of success. Keep an on-going list.

2. Measure manager, employee, and new hire attitudes toward and satisfaction with the process.

3. Determine the number of people passing through the process at each point in the process. You will need to provide frequencies and rates of flow.

4. Measure the cost to process a successful new hire. What does it cost to run the system (salaries, equipment, overhead, etc.)?

5. Measure input from managers, employees, and new hires on strengths, weaknesses, and recommended improvements for the system.

Do It

You already have been in the field collecting information to define the problem, create the research design, and measure the important indicators. Now you need to implement the surveys, locate the in-house data sources to complete your measures, and conduct the focus groups and key informant interviews.

Deliver It

Use the presentation strategies outlined in this chapter. In short:

1. Structure your report to meet the client's specifications.

2. Engage the client in the flowchart design or redesign, if this is appropriate.

3. Use transparencies or electronic presentation devices and software to present the three process designs: (a) what the process is, (b) what it currently is expected to be, and (c) what it could be.

4. Provide a bulleted outline of supporting descriptions and outcomes of the research and the proposed process.

5. Deliver a hard copy of the report in a manner appropriate to the corporate culture.

▧ Exercises

Here are a few exercises that will help you identify structure and the impact of change within a process. These exercises require a combination of life experiences and your understanding of process.

1. Select a process at the micro (self or person), meso (group/organizational), and macro (societal) levels. Identify a process at each level. Generally, describe the purpose of the process, that is, its function. What is it supposed to do? Now select one of these three and describe the flow through the process. What happens to somebody or something as it progresses through the process?

2. Select a process in which you currently participate. From "inside" process, diagram a flowchart that maps the elements of this system. Does the process tend to be linear and nonrecursive? Does it appear to cycle, that is, does it feed back on itself, and is it recursive? Consider the following: (a) Does the structure of the process have an impact on you? (b) If yes, describe how the process makes you feel, act, and/or think in a certain way.

3. Locate two processes that have been created in different groups or organizations to essentially do the same thing. For example, the process of raising young children in a family or in a day care center; the process of selling and distributing retail merchandise (cars, food, information); or the process of distributing education—it is your choice. Visit each of these groups. Describe and diagram the process for each. Now compare them. How are the structures different? How are they similar? Explain how the value systems and the corporate mission, goals, and objectives appear to have an impact on the outcome.

4. What is the impact of changing a process? In the newspaper, daily magazines, the Internet, or other media, select an example of a process that has been changed. For that process, describe (a) the nature of the process, (b) when and where it changed, and (c) the reason it changed. Now, and importantly, (d) describe the impact this change had at the macro, meso, and micro levels.

5. Select a process within any group or organization. Produce a plan for restructuring it. Diagram the old process. Using key informant interviews, collect information that will give you clues on how to modify or create a new version of the current process. Diagram the new process. Outline the differences between the old and the new processes. Why do you believe that the new process will be better than the old one? What impact would your change have on the people in the process

and on the functions that the process performs? What resistance would you expect to get from people living in this group?

6. Complete Exercise 5 above. Now create a brief proposal that outlines your recommended changes to the process, and present your findings to someone in authority in the group. Outline (a) the mission or purpose of the new process, (b) the goals and objectives you have for the new process, and (c) the action steps that you believe are necessary to enact your change. In addition, provide a diagram of the new process and your reasons for making the changes.

PART

*Lights,
Camera,
Action!*

Organizing the Group $\boxed{4}$

How often have you said, "Life is just too complicated"? As our society continues to reach higher levels of complexity, the number of tasks we must accomplish has also increased greatly. As these tasks have made life more complex, efforts to coordinate our activities have become more formalized. Today, most of our activities occur within formalized organizational settings. Among these are the stores where you purchase food and clothing, the schools you attend, the places where you work, the places you go for entertainment and worship, and so on. You cannot exist today without some contact with organizations.

When you need something done that requires the effort of more than one individual, a coordination of efforts represents a more efficient way to accomplish the work at hand. On the simplest level, the coordination may involve everyone doing the same thing. As the project becomes more complex, tasks are divided among individuals, each of whom plays a role in the overall completion of the work. Organizations therefore represent a structure in which a group has been organized to achieve specific goals by a coordinated, collective effort.

There are many different types of organizations, varying in terms of the goals they seek, their size, the formality of their structure, and their operating processes. How we view organizations can also vary. On one hand, organizations can be perceived as the logical and rational way to organize work. On the other hand, they can represent a loss of individual control, alienation, impersonal relationships, over-

The authors would like to recognize the substantive contributions of Joyce Iutcovich, President, Keystone University Research Corporation, on early versions of this chapter.

conformity, and a focus on means rather the goal of what needs to be accomplished.

Because organizations are systems of patterned interactions, we can change these patterns if we need to. Clearly, some organizations are easier to change than others, but the fact remains that we can redefine social reality. We can collectively decide how something should be, get people to collectively believe that it should be that way, and then get them to act accordingly.

Although organizations consist of people, they become a social entity unto themselves. This is a critical idea to understand; organizations are made up of people, but they also consist of elements that separate them from the people. Let us examine this in more detail. Suppose you want to buy a loaf of bread. It is highly unlikely that anyone in the organization of the supermarket opposes your purchase as long as you have the money to pay for it. What stands between you and the bread are a variety of organizational rules and processes. There are rules regarding when the store is open (time), where the store is located, what the store sells, how much the merchandise costs, and how one can pay for the merchandise. Although the people in the supermarket abide by these rules, they may not be responsible for creating them. In fact, they may be just as confused by some of the rules as you are.

The distribution and sale of bread to the supermarket relies on a system of interdependent operations and actions, both internal and external to the supermarket. The stocking of the shelves, the sale of the merchandise, and even the transaction between you and the clerks are structured by policy. Although these policies, rules, and norms are not human, they are perceived as being a living part of the organization.

Why is it important to study organizations? Because of their constant presence in our daily lives, many organizational structures fade into the background. We need to be reminded of their impact and be aware of how they interact with each other to maintain and keep our social system going. In today's rapidly changing society, to be successful and go beyond mere survival, it is important for us to understand the purpose of organizations, how they are designed, how they operate, and how they are changed.

Organizations, like any social thing, operate on at least three different levels. First, they create collective ways that the people in the organization use to view the world. This unique perspective is commonly called a corporate culture. Corporate cultures are ways of life within the organization (Schein, 1992). When you hear someone say,

"We do not do it that way around here," you are running up against the culture of the corporation.

Most corporate cultures have procedures on how to accomplish tasks, and they also have collective views of what is right or wrong. Additionally, most cultures have defining symbols (e.g., company logo), company heroes (such as Bill Gates at Microsoft®), and a corporate lore or history. When you become part of the organization, you are expected to learn and internalize the culture. Understanding this culture makes it easier to act with others in that organization and to achieve the organization's goals and objectives.

Second, organizations are social systems. In addition to the individual behavior necessary to make them go, organizations are made up of a number of interdependent parts. These parts exist within a social environment. Thus, the social system provides the place in which the tasks or functions can be accomplished. Remarkably, the functions may be known and clearly defined, or they may be totally unknown to the people who perform the tasks within them. As individuals pass through the system, they get linked up with and/or create interactions that further drive the system.

Third, and not surprisingly, you can expect conflict within organizations. Even though a system moves forward in some cultural environment, competing values, battles over scarce resources, and the use of power produce conflict within and between organizations. In a perfectly good organization that seems to be running fine, a vice president may arrive at work to find that his or her job has been eliminated, or the workers may arrive at the gate to find that the department was closed or the plant was shut down.

▨ The Problem of Restructuring

During the 1990s, a relatively new concept gained a lot of attention in the world of organizations and business. This concept, known as reengineering, defines a systematic evaluation of processes and resources in an attempt to make the organization run at peak efficiency. Sociologists view reengineering as a form of systematic social change. When this change occurs, three major things happen. First, the culture changes and influences the way things are done in the organization. Second, the changes in the overall culture change the ways in which individuals interact and perform within the culture. Third, these changes dictate the need for participants to be resocialized to the new rules, processes, and procedures.

Using these interdependent levels of change, let us look at an organizational phenomenon of the 1990s. Many large corporations have gone through a process known as downsizing. Downsizing, to some, is the removal of unnecessary tasks or functions from the business in order to lower costs and improve productivity. To others, downsizing is the politically correct way of saying that you are laying off or terminating a number of participants. No matter which perspective you take, downsizing is an example of social change. A change in any component of this social system will automatically ignite changes in all other components.

At least three things happen when a corporation downsizes. First, the system itself gets reorganized. Second, the organization usually reduces the number of participants. Third, the corporate culture changes in order to adapt to the new environment. It is important to remember that these changes in structure and processes actually cause the organization to evolve into a new, somewhat different system. From a sociological perspective, when reorganization occurs, the patterns of human interaction change. Presumably, this change is directed toward providing a better match between the social needs that the organization fills and its social "shape."

Organizational size and changing organizational complexity both have an impact through downsizing. The reduction in the labor force that usually accompanies downsizing simply reduces the number of people doing the work. The slack may be taken up by technology, overtime, and/or a redefinition of the way the work is divided up (division of labor). A middle manager may be eliminated in favor of a self-directed work team. A department of clerks may be exchanged for increased computer power. In either case, the result is fewer people and a series of changes in the system to adapt to the new environment. Regardless of the severity of the change, the nature of the organization changes, as do the human relationships within it. When this happens, the corporate culture changes.

Reorganization also changes the way of life within the organization. Old values and beliefs about work change. "The way things used to be" becomes a nostalgic dream. In this case, many people experience what sociologists call cultural lag. In cultural lag, the ways of the old culture do not change as quickly as needed to adapt to the new and emerging cultural norms and beliefs. This may appear to be a situation in which the head is detached from the body. New expectations for performance emerge, but people still cling to the old ways. This is expected, however, because people have learned the old ways and feel comfortable with them. The result is the need for resocialization.

Basically, people need to be rewired. They need to understand and become comfortable with the new ways of doing things. After a period of adjustment, most resocialized workers begin to feel more comfortable with and adapt to the new system. But resocialization is still necessary for those who cannot or will not learn the new system. One solution, for example, that is used to deal with downsizing is retirement. In this case, when an individual reaches retirement, the position he or she held is not refilled. In many organizations, this is further compounded by the offer of early retirement. Retirement is a major cultural change in most people's lives, and it requires resocialization. After going to work daily for most of your life, what do you do with the time you now have available? What if you were forced into early retirement and feel that you have a number of productive years still available?

Similarly, individuals who lose their jobs to downsizing have to go through a rather severe resocialization process. Not only do they have to face the reality of not having a job, they have to face both the short-term and long-term anxiety of wondering what they will do next and how they will support themselves and their families. To help with this transition, many companies offer an outplacement service that offers the individuals help in adjusting to the new role and finding a new position in another organization. This process is ongoing and requires resocialization in both the transition and after the new job is found, because the individuals going through this change are also going through a process of questioning and redefining themselves and their self-worth.

When reengineering and downsizing occur, the role of the applied sociologist becomes very valuable. Not only can the sociologist help to define the structure of the organization, but he or she can also predict the likely consequences that the restructuring process will produce. By anticipating the effects of the changes, the sociologist can help smooth the transition process by developing programs that will ameliorate some of the negative effects before they occur and lead to a more carefully conceived restructuring than would otherwise be possible.

▨ Giving an Organization Structure

All organizations represent collective efforts in the pursuit of specified goals. In this respect, organizations have a number of common elements: a social structure, a set of participants or actors, specified goals, defined technologies for transforming inputs into outputs, and an environment to which it must constantly adapt (Hall, 1987). The social structure refers to the routinized ways in which participants in an organization relate to one another. These patterned interactions consist of values, norms, and role expectations. An organization and its participants maintain values that are used as a guide in identifying goals and determining behavior. Thus, if we value health, our organization will be structured in such a way as to provide ways of maintaining our health and/or ridding us of disease.

Norms, or rules of behavior, are used to define appropriate ways to accomplish goals. Usually, these norms become a part of the organization's culture. When you hear someone say, "We do not do it that way around here," you are coming in direct contact with the culture of the organization. The behaviors appropriate for individuals occupying certain social positions within the organization are known as *role expectations*. A physician in a health care organization, for example, is expected to see patients and determine ways in which the patient can be treated for a health problem.

Sociologists have long discussed the linkage between the individual and the roles he or she performs. George Herbert Mead suggested that the development of the self was an interactive process, so the roles we play and the tasks we perform are firmly ingrained in how we view ourselves and our self-concept. But because our roles are tied to the larger organization, we may have little control over the new expectations. In fact, we may not be aware of or understand these expectations, or there may be no expectations at all.

Emile Durkheim, a French sociologist, warned us about what can happen when the social "rug" gets pulled out from under us. Durkheim suggested that people demonstrate a degree of personal pathology when their structure gets changed. This pathology can be in the form of anomie, or not knowing what is going to happen next or how to handle the situation. It can be in the form of alienation, where you feel disoriented or removed from the comfort of your role and the environment surrounding you. Finally, as Durkheim demonstrated, it can even elevate itself to the level of believing suicide to be the only solution to the problem.

Thus, the values, norms, and role expectations are all part of the organization's culture. Organizations have collective ways of doing things, collective views of right and wrong, defining symbols, and heroes. When you become a participant in the organization, you are expected to learn the organization's unique culture. Many of your actions (formally and informally) in the organization will be dictated or directed by the culture. But just like any other culture, the people who live it daily may be more or less socialized to that way of life.

An organization's social structure or culture is often viewed in terms of "what ought to be." The reality of most organizations, however, is that what actually exists may vary within the defined social structure. It is possible to find others who either do not know or are unwilling to accept the organization's culture or way of life. So, like other cultures, deviance and conflict exist within organizations, often in patterned ways. Even though the organization moves along according to a set of cultural traditions, there may be competing values and battles over scarce resources and the use of power. In an organization that seems to be working fine, a vice president may arrive at work to find that her computer password is not recognized and she no longer has access to company files. This may be a glitch in the computer, but more likely, it is the company's culture telling the vice president that she no longer has a job.

The organizational participants are those individuals who carry out the plans and activities of the organization. They must be induced to make their contributions because the extent and intensity of their involvement can vary tremendously. Participants are the primary elements of the organization and are the vehicle through which organizations operate and change. Without them, there is no organization, no social structure, no culture, and no activity. But because a participant's involvement can range from the insignificant (an occasional visitor) to the prime mover (the chief executive officer of a large corporation), the extent to which the personal characteristics of individuals can affect the functioning of the organization can also vary dramatically. Thus, both the status and the personality characteristics of the contributors within an organization are important factors to consider when analyzing the design and operation of an organization.

Conceptions of what the organization wants to accomplish represent a way of defining goals. These goals are the reasons that organizations are established in the first place; that is, to coordinate the activities of the participants so that the organization's objectives can be achieved.

Although this sounds very straightforward, the notion of goals and the function they serve can be very controversial. In some cases, organizations specify goals in order to justify past behavior. At other times, the individuals within the organization create their own goals, which may or may not be compatible with the overall organizational goals. In a large number of cases, the real goals of the organization may differ greatly from the stated goals.

The technologies for transforming inputs into outputs consist of more than just machinery or mechanical equipment. The technological skills and knowledge of the participants represent channels through which the work of the organization is accomplished. Thus, the process for carrying out the work of an organization can be defined as its technology. In some organizations, this technology may be poorly understood, outdated, inefficient, or haphazardly applied. In other organizations, the technology used is considered state of the art. Given the rapid changes in the workplace and organizations, it is essential for organizations to constantly assess and upgrade the effectiveness of their technological base if they are to survive in today's society.

Finally, organizations do not exist in a vacuum. They are part of other systems and must constantly adapt to the changes that occur in their physical, social, and cultural environments. There is interdependence between an organization and its environment; that is, not only are the structures and operations of the organization influenced by the environment, but the organization, in turn, strongly influences the environment around it. Organizational participants come with their own socialization and training experiences that influence the activities of the organization. But at the same time, the activities of the organization (e.g., downsizing) can directly affect the lives of the participants.

☒ Research Tools

Studying the organization can run the gamut from obtaining literature on the organization and performing secondary analysis to a direct on-site investigation of the organization's structure and processes. Each technique will offer unique insights into the organization, such as a perspective on the organization's culture, whether it be ideal (printed statements) or real (what people actually do). However, individual techniques may be limiting in that they focus on only one area or view of the organization. For this reason, it is best that the researcher use a combination of techniques whenever possible. This process is called triangulation and, as the name suggests, it presents a number of different views of the phenomenon in order to get a more accurate picture of it.

Probably one of the easiest ways to gather information on an organization is through the information that the organization generates about itself or that is written about it. Normally, the larger and more visible the organization, the greater the amount of information available and the easier it is to access it. Social agencies and larger public businesses are required by law to make certain information available to the public. Many times, this is in the form of an annual report or other documents on the current health of the organization. These reports will normally tell you what the organization is about, who it serves, and what it identifies as its goals and objectives. Remember, however, that these documents are usually written or approved by the organization and are usually prepared to put the organization in the best possible light. Thus, it is important to obtain information from other nonrelated sources, such as newspaper and magazine articles. These articles will help to place the organization in a broader arena and allow you to gain an understanding of how the community views the organization.

A second way of gathering information on an organization is to survey individuals who work directly with the organization. This may be other agencies or businesses that have daily contact with the organization under investigation. In business, these types of interviews are called customer satisfaction surveys. They can be done through one-on-one interviews, surveys (telephone or mailed), or even focus groups. Keep in mind that each of these techniques will have different costs and will be limited in getting the information you desire. This especially holds true if you are trying to contact senior management in the other organizations. Telephone calls may not be returned, and mail surveys may end up in the trash. Thus, it is important that you figure out the best way to interview the appropriate people in a timely and cost-efficient manner.

A third way of examining an organization is to talk directly with the members of the organization. This can be done through surveys or, if the situation allows, on-site direct interaction with the members. By being on-site and a part of the day-to-day workings of the organization, you will be able to judge how well the organization's structure and processes are working. Keep in mind, however, that by just being there, you may disrupt the normal activities, and the members may be prone to tell you what they think you want to hear (social desirability bias) for fear that the information given may affect their status in the organization.

Thus, the organization can and should be examined at a number of levels using a number of different techniques. The use of multiple techniques should help to cross-validate information received, and it should identify and minimize any biases that occur during the research. A word on ethics is important here. As mentioned earlier, organizations are made up of people, and these individuals have personal rights, such as privacy and job security (i.e., sociologists should not engage in research or activities that put an employee's privacy or job in jeopardy). When studying organizational behavior, like all other social behavior, it is important that the researcher be aware of potential areas where less than ethical behavior could occur (e.g., breaking confidentiality, stealing data, sharing unauthorized findings) and assure the client that everything will be done to minimize the potential for this behavior. The researcher has a moral obligation to protect the client and other participants and, as hard as it may be, must remove him- or herself from the project if the ethics are compromised. Not only is this the ethically right thing to do, it is also the safest from a legal standpoint.

▨ Presentation Tools

Most organizations, especially businesses, make decisions at a very rapid pace. Before these decisions can be made, however, information must be disseminated in a meaningful manner to a number of participants, each with different levels of experience and interest. There are a few simple guidelines you can follow that will help make your presentation more actionable and, at the same time, enhance your role as an applied sociologist.

Know Your Audience

As mentioned earlier, organizations are made up of diverse groups of individuals. These individuals have different statuses in the organization, play out different roles, have different educational and experiential backgrounds, and, most importantly, have different levels of interest in the subject being presented. You may be required to speak to the entire group at one time or to a number of smaller, more focused, groups. In either case, you will be better prepared if you take the time to learn something about the "hot buttons," or key areas of interest, for each group. This will allow you to hold their attention and give them information they can use immediately.

One of the authors once gave a presentation to a group of engineers. Assuming that they were well-versed in multivariate statistical techniques, the presentation consisted of an elaborate regression model. Within the first 5 minutes of the presentation, the presenter noticed a majority of the audience looking confused. Upon asking about the confusion, the presenter was informed that everyone in the audience used simple measures of variance and percentages, and no one had any idea what he was talking about.

Keep It Simple

Presentations exist to inform the audience about your key findings. The audience usually does not have the time or inclination to want to sit and listen to someone reading a report to them word for word. If they want to read the entire report, they will do it when it is convenient for them. More likely, however, they will be interested in only those findings that are directly related to them or their jobs.

Good presentations usually include a small number of relevant slides or transparencies that give the audience short "sound-bite" pieces of information that they can internalize quickly. With this in mind, the presentation format should include only one or two key findings per page. Make these findings easy to read (many people use bullets) and do not overload the slide with a lot of supporting material. Use the speaking part of your presentation to add the additional, supportive information. Where it makes sense, use uncomplicated charts, graphs, and pictures to help make your point.

Above all, make sure the presentation is alive, flowing, and interesting. Your results may be earth-shattering, but if the audience is asleep or daydreaming, they will never get the message. Professional presenters follow the K.I.S.S. rule: Keep It Simple, Stupid.

Differentiate Fact From Fiction

There will be at least one member of the audience who will say, "I always thought . . . " or "They say . . . " about the point you are making. The problem with these statements is that they are usually based on hearsay and not scientific research and analysis. This may be the hardest part of making the presentation. How do you change someone's perception without making them feel foolish, embarrassed, or insulted? The best way to do this is to courteously show how the facts differ from the perception. Never belittle the individual or make him or her look foolish in front of the group. Your goal is not to show the audience how much you know but to give them accurate information that they can understand and use.

Be Prepared for Difference of Opinion

It is inevitable that at least some of the audience will not agree with your findings. When this happens, attempt to find out (a) whether they fully understand your findings, (b) whether they have additional information that lends credence to their opinion, or (c) whether they just refuse to accept or believe your findings. If the difference is over a misunderstanding of the results, a simple review may remedy the situation. If the discrepancy is over information that you did not have, then you will have to quickly assess whether the new information is feasible and accurate, and whether it affects your findings. Do not be afraid to say that you will study this new information and revise your findings if needed.

Finally, if the difference of opinion is based on a refusal to accept your findings, you will have to quickly assess the situation to see whether the disagreement is with one or two people or the entire audience. If it is with an individual, try to diffuse the confrontation immediately by saying that it might be best to have a personal discussion after the presentation. If this does not work, move on to the next subject. You do not want to risk alienating your entire audience just to prove yourself to one individual. However, if the entire audience is in disagreement, you will want to facilitate a discussion on why they feel the way they do. Remember, they are your clients, and if they do not accept the findings, no matter how accurate or how much work you put into them, they will not implement them.

Be Prepared to Do Further Research and Analysis

Most good presentations will generate as many questions as answers. Try to successfully answer as many questions as possible during the presentation. If there are questions that you cannot answer, tell the client that you will be happy to go back to your data and try to find the answer. This suggests to the audience that you are willing to work with them, and you have their best interests in mind.

▨ Sociologist as Expert

Individuals skilled in applied sociology have the ability to become excellent strategists and planners. After all, planning requires an understanding of social systems, social processes, and social change. To construct a plan, you must have some knowledge of the social environment in which that plan will be carried out. This environment could range from a small group or task team on the microscopic level to a large global company or society at the macroscopic level. All of this requires taking a comprehensive view of the structure of the group, the roles that individuals play within the structure, and the possible outcomes of the strategies selected.

If you were asked, for example, to prepare an educational strategic plan, it would not do you much good to focus on education alone without also looking at changes in technology, population (e.g., changing number and diversity of students), as well as changes in other, related social institutions, such as business, government, religion, and the family. Time must also be taken into consideration. You will need to understand the social forces that affected the situation in the past and the present. More importantly, you will need to be able to predict the types and levels of intensity of the social forces that will influence the organization into the future. Sociologists are trained to identify and interpret emerging trends and social change and, therefore, to see the world from a broad perspective.

Strategic planning is a natural role for sociologists to play. They have been trained in logical thinking and disciplined inquiry. These elements form the basic foundation of most actionable plans. Let us look at the components of a strategic plan and see how applied sociology can be beneficial.

By definition, a plan is "the process of determining what [something] intends to be in the future and how it will get there" (Barry, 1986, p. 10). Breaking down this definition, we see that, first of all, planning is a *process*. It views organizational behavior as dynamic and changing. The process calls for the setting of goals or objectives to be achieved. These goals become the benchmarks on which the success or failure of the plan is measured. Next, for each of these goals or objectives, strategies are defined. These strategies should be viewed as the overall route one plans to take to achieve the goals. Finally, each strategy is broken down into a series of steps or tactical plans that need to be completed to make the strategy a success.

To do this, we must do some envisioning, which is

> the process by which individuals or groups develop a vision or dream of a future state for themselves or their organizations that is both sufficiently clear and powerful to arouse and sustain the actions necessary for that dream or vision to become a reality. (Goodstein et al., 1993, p. 38)

Many people struggle with this notion of vision because it seems very abstract and hard to measure. Reaching group consensus on a vision requires an integration of trend analysis and group process, along with the need to do an environmental scan in which all social forces are defined within the environment. Applied sociologists have the training and knowledge to do this quickly and accurately. By doing so, we create a complete scenario of how things are and what they are likely to be.

Again, we refer to a "social construction of reality" (Berger & Luckmann, 1966). It is created or constructed socially through interaction with other individuals. Once constructed, it becomes real as the individuals within the group or organization approve of and follow it. Simply stated, plans are artificially created by individuals, and they become real when the group follows them. But before we can construct present reality or predict the future, we need to be able to answer some very important questions.

- What is the group's or organization's purpose or mission?
- Why does it exist?
- Who is the audience(s)?
- What does the group or organization expect to do for or to this audience?
- What is the group's or organization's vision for the future?
- Where does the group see itself in 3 to 5 years?
- Currently, how far removed is the group from the vision?
- What factors might stop it from realizing the vision?
- Which structural factors (social, political, economic, cultural, etc.) or issues will have to be overcome before the vision can be achieved?
- Which resources (human, financial) are currently available, and what will be needed to achieve the vision?

- How will the group or organization be structured or mobilized to achieve their goals and visions?

All of these questions have a "sociologic" commonality: They are all made by and for humans. They are the components needed to socially construct reality. Regardless of what we are planning, we will need to set strategies and then produce a set of steps (plans) in order to respond to each of these items and move successfully into the future.

▧ Case Study

The Case

A social agency in your community has decided to develop a strategic plan for its organization for the next 3 years. The agency assists victims of crimes with both their physical and legal needs. As such, this group usually arrives on the crime scene shortly after the police and begins immediately to comfort the victims and attend to their most pressing needs. The agency then develops a plan to help the victims obtain the needed resources (food, clothing, shelter) and then follows up with the victims to make sure that they are eventually overcoming the trauma of being victimized.

This is a public agency, and it is required by its funding agencies to develop and implement a 3-year program to show how the funding will be spent to achieve these goals. As an applied sociologist, you have been hired to help them put this plan together. How would you go about developing the strategic plan?

Possible Solutions

1. Background

- Find out everything you can about the community and the clients whom the agency serves.
  a. How big is the community, and what is its level of victimization?
  b. Who are the individuals who are usually victimized in the community?
  c. Historically, who has used the agency's services? What are the social, economic, and demographic factors associated with these individuals?

    d. Are there any political issues related to victimization and this agency
       in the community?
  • Develop a brief profile of the agency.
    a. When did it start? Who started it? Was or is it affiliated with other
       organizations (e.g., religious groups) in the community?
    b. What is the agency's stated mission and vision?
    c. Where are they at in achieving their stated mission and goals?
    d. What resources does the agency have available (human, financial,
       physical) to help them achieve their goals? What resources will they
       need?

2. Developing the plan

  • Doing preliminary research
    a. Set up a meeting with the management of the agency.
    b. Ask and obtain all relevant information from the agency.
    c. After you have had a chance to digest the information, ask manage-
       ment and key staff questions about the information.
    d. Begin to note whether the ideal culture of the agency differs from the
       real one.
  • Doing primary research
    a. Based on the notes you have gathered above, develop and implement
       a survey of individuals from each of the following groups: senior
       management, staff/workers, and clients.
    b. While interviewing the various groups, ascertain whether there is a
       shared perspective of the problem and the agency's philosophy on
       how to remedy it. Do perspectives differ between and among the
       groups studied?

3. Writing the plan

  • Find a format that the agency understands and with which it is comfort-
    able. There are numerous strategic planning formats available from
    which to choose.
  • Work closely with the management team to make sure they approve and
    buy into your findings and recommendations.
  • At minimum, make sure the plan addresses the following:
    a. The agency's mission (i.e., who they perceive themselves to be, who
       their clients are, and how they will successfully serve their clients)
    b. The agency's vision for the next 3 years (where they want to be)
    c. Key trends and issues affecting the agency and its goals
    d. An assessment of where the agency is at present
    e. Clearly defined, mutually agreed upon goals and objectives

f. Strategies needed to achieve these goals

g. Specific plans or programs that will be developed to support the strategies

h. The resources needed, be they human or financial, to achieve all of the above

An actual strategic plan will encompass most or all of the factors discussed above. The key job of the planner is to make sure that the plan actually meets the needs of the agency and is achievable if followed. In this sense, the strategic planner is as much a facilitator/moderator as he or she is a researcher.

Exercises

1. Select an organization in which you are interested and obtain a copy of their organizational chart. This chart should show the chain of command from the leader down to the other members of the organization. For a large organization, these charts can become very complex, so you might want to start with a smaller organization, such as your church or a local social agency. Once you have the chart:

- Examine it and attempt to understand how the organization is structured. What are the key leadership positions? How are the major tasks or functions divided?

- Next, identify individuals at various levels in the structure and attempt to interview them. Ask them questions about the organization's structure and their role in it. More specifically, ask them how they personally perceive the structure. In their view, is the structure really like it looks on paper? Do the power and authority really flow from the top down through the ranks? You may find that there is an ideal structure (the organizational chart) and a real structure (i.e., key individuals in the middle of the structure with a substantial amount of power and influence).

2. Select an organization and identify the key elements of its culture. First of all, gather any information that the organization sends out as public relations material (e.g., annual reports, flyers, philosophy/values statements, speeches). Using this information, list any factors that would seem to be indicators of how the organization acts and thinks. These factors are usually found in mission statements, vision statements, statements about the organization's philosophy or values,

and state-of-the-organization speeches given to the members and other
interested parties. Once you have developed a profile of the culture,
interview some of its members to determine

- Whether your perception of the culture is correct
- Whether the members are aware of the organization's stated culture
- Whether the organization says one thing while the members do some-
  thing else

Once again, you may find that there is an ideal organizational culture
and a real culture, which are very different from each other.

   3. Find a major company that went through downsizing in the
early 1990s. Do some library or on-line research to find newspaper and
magazine articles written at the time of the downsizing that noted some
of the major issues and impacts of the downsizing. Next, gather current
information on the company to ascertain what the long-term effects of
this process have been. In your opinion, has the company benefited
from the downsizing? Why or why not?

Leading the Pack: Strategies for Leadership

Leadership is an important issue in applied settings. The active nature of applied work suggests that sociologists could easily be "out in front" of others. In this chapter, we will show that the sociological perspective and the elements of sociological training can be used effectively to create leaders. In many respects, sociology has had latent potential in this area. Knowing how society and human relationships work should enhance the potential for leaders to emerge.

⚙ Moving to the Front of the Pack

Leadership is a key issue in applied sociology. There are at least two reasons. First, applied sociologists can assist and direct clients to set a clear course for action. In a rapidly changing social situation, this can be extremely valuable. Assisting in the creation of leaders, leading organizations and programs are of great significance. Second, leadership requires process and structure across a wide range of social activity. In this chapter, we will look at the connection of sociological concepts to the processes of leading and leadership. To do this, we must view leadership across a broad spectrum of sociological information. We will link leadership to microlevel and highly personal concepts, such as "self," as well as to macrolevel concepts, such as "social change." This is due to the fact that the characteristics of what constitutes leadership cut across the entire spectrum of social life. Leadership is dynamic, and to this end, we will venture a relatively simple but powerful approach to leadership: In short, leaders demonstrate "moraling, modeling, and molding." Let us discuss these three processes.

Contemporary leadership author and consultant Warren Bennis has greatly advanced the quest to understand leadership. A review of his work, and that of sociologists such as Max Weber and Emile Durkheim, plus other contemporary writers, leads us to three major elements of leadership that, when taken together, drive the creation of leaders. Leaders are grounded; they provide structure in the midst of chaos and change. They are able to do this because they have forged and internalized a system of personal and social beliefs, values, and norms that provides a structured route to follow. The process of envisioning this personal and social structure tied to a belief system is what we mean by *moraling*. A good sense of personal identity and a dynamic understanding of self are essential. This structure transcends the present and the past and must be projected into the future. Moraling means actively creating a plausible reality complete with norms, values, and beliefs. As a system, this provides an organized path for people to follow.

Hence, leaders are capable of acting in anomic situations. The sociologist Emile Durkheim (1951) explained that anomie is a social situation that is normless. Rapidly changing society gives this impression. No sooner do we institute a structure to deal with a social need than we find that the need changes or the structure becomes inoperative. We see norms challenged on a variety of fronts. A leader supplies a workable plan of action to confront what may appear as chaos. Durkheim researched the impact of the normlessness that emerges when the social rug is pulled out from under people—when patterns on which we rely suddenly disappear.

A leader can respond to this. In fact, leaders are perhaps at their best under these conditions. Business luminary Tom Peters (1988) deals with just this response to disorder in his book *Thriving on Chaos*. This book is an insightful depository of creative, courageous, and even heroic responses to chaotic social conditions. Among these examples are people and organizations that laid down a path where none existed. In this way, someone set the agenda for a solution. A leader is capable of creating structure. Applied sociologists take note: This could be you! One word of caution: Just as moths are attracted to light, humans are attracted to structure. We would like to take the bridge that leads us over turbulence, but unfortunately, we might end up in a world in which we do not wish to be. When humans choose a bridge to carry them in their social life, they not only walk on the bridge, but they also become the bridge. When leaders provide structure and humans follow that structure, the followers take on the characteristics of the structure, knowingly or unknowingly. Anomic conditions produce an environment in which followers sacrifice personal freedom for structure. The result may be horrendous or extraordinary. Adolf Hitler's vision for Germany and the structure presented therein demonstrated such a terrifying response to an anomic condition. Conversely, John F. Kennedy's vision of landing a man on the moon by the end of the 1960s was a vision and structure that superseded his tragic death in 1963. Applied sociologists in support of leaders, and as leaders themselves, must tread with caution.

Essential to this moraling process is developing a clear vision of the future. Leaders must be able to conceptualize the future and extend the present into it in a plausible manner. By this, we are not suggesting a fortune teller, nor even a forecaster. Rather, a leader needs to look down the road, scan the environment, take a hard focus, and create an image of just where the group ought to be going. This is where the applied sociologist needs to be a futurist. Art Shostak, a prominent contemporary practicing sociologist, shares our concern for the lack of future thinking among sociologists. Shostak (1988, pp. 33-34) points out that sociology has long had the vision and the tools for assisting society with a future view. He quotes first American Sociological Association President Lester Ward's first presidential address, in 1906, in which Ward laid the groundwork for sociologists as futurist and policy leaders:

> Sociology has now begun, not only in some degree to forecast the future of society, but to venture suggestions as to how the established principles of the science may be applied to the future advantageous modifications of existing social structures. In other words, sociology, established as pure science, is now entering upon its applied stage, which is the great practical object for which it exists. (Ward, 1907, p. 9)

Let us devote some thought to this part of the applied sociologist's role. We all have an interest in the future. We act in the present with the input from the past in anticipation of the future. Many professionals study the future, and sociologists are well suited for this future view. After all, we spend much of our time attempting to track social change. We often investigate the nature of social forces that shape contemporary society, and we often hypothesize about likely outcomes, which may result from the variables that we measure in our research. Taking this analysis into the future is, perhaps, the ultimate applied problem. Leaders must draw as accurate a picture of the future as they can in order to envision how their plan of action will connect the present and the future. Although no one can predict the future with 100% accuracy, we can make a serious effort to construct some likely futures. These scenarios are stories about the way the world is likely to be. Notice that "scenarios" is plural. We create multiple scenarios—more than one future is possible. Scenario writing draws on a group's or individual's approach to the future. It also draws on qualitative and quantitative skills, as well as science and art. Let us explain further. Ackoff (1981) contends that there are four ways to approach planning for the future. First, we can take a reactive approach. Leaders who take this approach envision the future as an extension of the past. If you want to know what is happening tomorrow, next week, or 10 years from now, just look behind you! Scenarios for this type of future reflect the trends of the past. For example, if the rate of use of a health care facility has been growing over the past 10 years, we project growth for the next 10. We write a scenario for the future, which is different from today in terms of this increased use. The reactive leader may be compared to one who is relatively inactive in planning for the future. This approach allows an organization to flow on the surface of the status quo. The forces of contemporary society will chart direction. The future is not anticipated to any great extent. The other two perspectives for future planning are more dynamic.

Preactive future planners monitor the environment for emerging trends. Through environmental scanning, they are sensitized to emerging trends and changing social forces. These leaders recognize the dynamic nature of such trends and act to position themselves or their organizations in such a way as to maximize the benefit gained from these forces. In earlier chapters, we addressed strategic planning, and for the most part, strategic planning is preactive futures planning. If you want your organization to be carried forward by the force of a wave of change, put your organization in the best place to "catch the wave!"

Now, what if you decide that you not only want to maximize your positioning to get the best social wave, but you also want to take action to increase your synergy with it? You want to use your personal or organizational energy in the most dynamic interaction possible with emerging trends. You want a real synthesis! You would be a proactive leader, in Ackoff's terms. Proactivity implies a critical mass of energy resulting in synergy (some new form). Writing a scenario around this type of future planning is difficult. It produces results for which nothing has ever existed quite like it before. A true metamorphosis occurs; there is a bold transformation.

Finally, in moraling, leaders need to take a macro perspective. What is happening in the grand scheme of things? Can we extend the vision to the general levels of life? If any professionals are capable of "thinking globally and acting locally," it should be sociologists! Our entire perspective, even at the micro level, reflects a vision of human life from the top down. We are system thinkers, ever setting the nature of the domain in which people live, and then making generalizations about the impact of the forces around us. Practicing sociologists recognize the value of this perspective in dealing with clients. A macro view can turn the tables on narrow-mindedness and atomistic thinking. Leaders must see the big picture, and sociologists are capable of drawing that picture. Let us take an example of the value of the macro view.

If you think you are busy today, just wait until tomorrow! Things are more likely to move faster! Humankind has developed rapidly over the past 1,000 years. To make sense of what is going on, sociology teaches us to "get to the high ground" and look down on the situation. From this perspective, we can, as the World Future Society suggests, "think globally and act locally." As Daniel Bell (1973) pointed out, where humans have been and what they do has changed markedly. Human societies have moved from preindustrial societies (hunting and gathering societies) to agricultural societies to industrial societies to the postindustrial society in which we currently live, in a relatively short period of time. The transfer to the postindustrial society brought with it a major transition. Information creation and distribution became central to these societies. Technology to support information development emerged rapidly in the second half of the 20th century. Humans in these societies create symbols such as words, ideas, and things that stand for other things. They create symbolic realities in which they live. Through all of this, the velocity of change increases.

Where does grounding in a belief system fit? Throughout these periods of societal transition, many things have changed, but for now, let us look at the relationship of humans to time and space. This may sound like an unnecessary leap into abstraction, but take a minute to recognize the value of human connections to time and space. What you are doing right now is very much grounded in where and when you are doing it. For hunters and gatherers in preindustrial societies, it was essential to synchronize (line up) their lives with the cycles of the seasons, animals, and plants on which they relied. These cycles meant changing places to conform to changes in points along a cycle. Defining time, space, and social activity in light of Mother Earth was a plausible relationship. Although humans extended more control over the environment in agricultural societies, the direct dependence on being in a place in which crops could grow at the right time (seasons) was a core determinant of patterns of human life. In short, people had to be in the right place at the right time to have a chance at successful existence.

Industrial societies shifted the location of activity to human-created environments. Factories and production schedules dominated time and place for human social life. Ultimately, everything from automobiles to hamburgers, from newspapers to education, was produced in these systems. The process of manufacturing or of service delivery required attendance to a synchronization of humans with the time and place of work or service delivery. Patterns of social life were synchronized to bureaucratic time schedules in fixed locations.

But what about today? Although much of our lives are still governed by fixed time-and-space systems, we are seeing the emergence of life, which, as Microsoft computer magnate Bill Gates says, is "asynchronous." The information society makes it possible to leave e-mail, do business, contact your bank, and create the products of the post-industrial society just about any time you want. Cellular phones, beepers, the Internet, and the World Wide Web are just some of the devices that make it possible to live on a more person-centered schedule. We are not suggesting that we are free to do whatever we want, but we are more likely to do what we are doing at a variety of times and places. Teachers and students, physicians and patients, employers and workers—none of these familiar role sets requires a synchronized place and time for a social interaction to occur. The definitions of the relationships have changed and are changing. Time and space have been altered radically. The challenge to modern leaders is the challenge of belief systems—moraling in the grand scheme of things.

As you can see, standing on the high ground and looking down is an important ability. This macro vision is also important when we look into the distance, into the future, and attempt to determine the shape of what we see. Leaders and leadership demand this view.

Now, let us turn to modeling. Leaders must understand the relationship between self and others. The results of leadership may be experienced at a level beyond the individual leader, but leadership is transferred at the micro level: Leaders lead people. Their social visions, their structure for the present and the future, as well as their plans, must be delivered person to person, self to self. We necessarily must transfer our view at the level of the individual—the self. Although leaders need to know who they are, they must also be able to demonstrate this to others. As applied sociologists, we can use tools supplied by George Herbert Mead (1934). Mead explained the nature of the self as a dynamic interplay of the "I" and the "Me"—the unique and the social. The outcome is a "self." For Mead, human interactions really are not human (as opposed to what other animals do) until we are able to take in the expectations of others. This makes us social—humanly social.

Here, Bennis reminds us that leaders "accept responsibility," and that "true understanding [comes] from reflecting on [your] experience" (Bennis, 1989, p. 56). Like all of us, leaders develop self-concepts (ideas about who we are) and self-esteem (the value we have for ourselves) from the self-creating process outlined by Mead. Much of what we learn to do is expressed through role playing and role taking. Each role is a unique blend of the unique portion of self, the "I," and the set of expectations and obligations that we take in from others, the "Me." To be a leader, one needs to act like a leader. This modeling does two things. First, it sets up a self-fulfilling prophecy. Leaders are leaders, in part, because they believe they are! Second, others may understand and contribute to this notion.

In *Learning to Lead* (Bennis & Goldsmith, 1994), leadership authority Warren Bennis summarizes some valuable characteristics of a leader. In short, he says that a leader needs to demonstrate "constancy, congruity, reliability and integrity" (1994, pp. 132-134). Leaders need to be trusted (constancy). They are the ones with the visions, and they are the ones who stay the course. Furthermore, leaders "walk their talk." They act in accordance with their vision, and they do what they say they plan to do (congruity). They can be counted on by those whom they lead (reliability), and they honor their commitments and promises (integrity). These characteristics may be expressed in a variety of ways. For example, some leaders are characterized as expressive. Expressive leaders set strong socioemotional direction. They understand the collective personal nature of those whom they must lead. In contrast, instrumental leaders are able to structure and complete tasks. Not surprisingly, a combination of these characteristics (expressive and instrumental) would produce a sensitive, understanding leader who could get the job done—a potent combination. The preference for one type of leadership over another may well be a unique, individual characteristic, perhaps guided by the way we see the world. This may very well be, in part, a psychological determination. For example, we often associate instrumental leaders with left-brain thinking and socioemotional leaders with right-brain thinking. Ideally, we would prefer leaders who think with both sides of their brain! However, we can also combine this with what people learn. And, of course, we believe that leaders can be made!

Finally, let us turn to molding. Sociologists are very likely to maintain that leaders are made, not born. This is where we contend that leadership can be learned. We can socialize people to think of themselves as leaders and/or followers. When we take roles, we internalize the expectations that go along with that role. In other words, we take into ourselves these social forms from outside. A role is a vehicle, a personal and social vehicle. A vehicle is something that enables you to get from one place to another. This vehicle does at least three things: (a) It lets you know what to do, (b) it funnels your personal energy into the society, and (c) it contributes to the shape of who you are. In short, it is a way to get you "hooked up" with society while you supply the energy to make collective social life (the patterns of human interaction) go. On the personal side, the self side, it influences who you are. Notice also that roles come from two external directions. There are some roles over which you do not have much control. Before you had a chance, somebody else labeled you a "boy" or a "girl," and then this became a signal for a flood of things to happen that shaped who you are. These kinds of roles are called ascribed roles. On the other hand, there are some roles that you choose, such as "worker" or "student." Because you chose them, we call them achieved roles. Here enters the self-fulfilling prophecy. Naturally, we can think of leadership roles that are ascribed, but leadership can be achieved. We can and do make leaders. To mold leaders, we set expectations for those roles, and then we ask people to take them.

Creating leaders means taking the role of the other. Creating leaders has a great deal to do with human interaction. How we feel about our worth, how we think about ourselves, and whether we see ourselves as leaders or followers can be influenced strongly by the expectations of others. Your decision to be a leader may be predicated by your relationship to others. These may be people whom you know (significant others, in George Mead's terms), and people whom you do not know—generalized others. When you say, "Society expects me to be a leader," you are talking about a general thing—society—not someone, but everyone. You do not really know everyone, but that is all right because you still act like you do! It works. As the sociologist Charles Horton Cooley (1902) said, our selves are "looking glass" selves: We look in a social mirror and see ourselves as we perceive others see us.

If you look in this social mirror and begin to see a follower, that may become your self-concept. Your idea of yourself is that of a follower, and it should not surprise you that you will act that way. The opposite is true as well. If we actively socialize people to be leaders, we are likely to create those who envision themselves that way. Leaders have this worked out! They know who they are in relationship to others. They can develop a vision and take responsibility for it. We can readily see the impact of ascribed roles in determining who may be viewed as a leader. To be a leader, there needs to be someone committed to beliefs, behavior, and characteristics, which that leader provides.

Leaders must get people to commit to the vision; they must get people to follow them! Of course, this may be through coercion or by choice, or both! Regardless, leaders are in constant interaction with their environment. They are dynamic, but they are simultaneously embedded in the world of others. Hence, leaders are able to empathize with others. They can take the role of others. This is valuable in understanding the needs and values of those who will be led. Using the symbolic interactionist view, a leader is able to enter and understand the life-worlds of others. Leaders know where they are coming from because they have made an effort to understand the definition of reality that is operative.

Applied sociologists are routinely trained to do many of the things that leaders must do. Let us review some of the leadership tools that are already a portion of the general training of sociologists and that translate into potential leadership skills.

▓ Effective Communication Skills

Business leader Phil Crosby (1996) highlights the importance of a leader expressing her or his vision in clear, direct, short statements. Unfortunately, common training in sociology often requires students to write and express themselves in a manner that is not clear to the public (and, often, not even to other sociologists). Much of sociology is jargon-laden and, hence, nearly impossible to decipher. Strong oral and written skills are essential. The ability to tie up complicated thoughts in a clear, direct manner is central. This is a precarious balance. Leaders must understand others without conforming to social pressure when the vision is challenged. The work of classic theorist Emile Durkheim is useful here. Leaders may become completely part of the society that they lead (to some degree like Durkheim's altruism). In Mead's terms, they become the vision (the "Me" part of the self). They become the society. This is potent, but it erases the value of the personal uniqueness that may be necessary to gain perspective on a problem. On the other extreme, leaders may cut themselves off, or find themselves cut off, from the interaction of others. They often need to make difficult decisions without the support of others—decision in a vacuum (egoistic situation). Although this personal courage is essential, remaining detached from others isolates one from the collective world of those who must be led. Combining these approaches with the expressive-instrumental characteristics we mentioned earlier, we can conceptualize the nature of interaction with others and the type of leadership needed on at least two dimensions. In this model, the most dynamic leader is one who can get a job done while understanding those whom he or she leads. In addition, he or she provides direction and commitment in supporting and promoting the group's vision but can make the tough choices necessary to keep the organization moving toward a desired outcome.

☙ Research Tools

The theoretic perspectives in sociology are valuable leadership tools. In the process of creating a vision for the future, a leader can use a functionalist or systems view of the nature of society. By doing this, he or she sees a society that transforms itself in the future by adapting to its environment. Changes will be enacted to align with need, both internal and external, to the society as well as to the organization or project that one is leading. The interdependent nature of the parts of the organization and its relationship to the world around it suggest a dynamic undulation. Systems are formed and reformed as the organization seeks balance. The transformation of the structure of the American automobile is an example. The car's engine size, number of occupants, and fuel economy all evolved through the interplay of economic, social, technological, and environmental forces. Writing scenarios for this leader relies on an understanding of complex interactions.

If we use conflict tools to shape our future scenario, we may end up with a different picture. The conflict view resembles a proactive planning strategy. Remember, conflict is not necessarily wrong. When conflict occurs, that is, when two or more social forces collide, energy is released and new social forms emerge. The resulting synthesis may not resemble anything that has preceded it. The emergence of the computer chip is an invention of this kind, but so is the bureaucracy or changing attitudes toward civil rights. The synergy produced by the impact of changing gender roles, declining birth rates, efficient transportation systems, and bureaucratized restaurants likely produced the type of social fusion necessary for the emergence of the drive-through window at a fast-food restaurant. Scenario writing may be very difficult under these circumstances. If, on the other hand, we take an interactionist perspective on the future, we will write a scenario in which the world will become what it is collectively defined to be. Reality construction is the product of action between humans. Defining the symbols we use to make sense of reality allows us to make up the world in which we live and then live in it! Emerging definitions are the content of such future scenarios.

We are likely to get a more detailed vision of the future if we use all three of these perspectives to provide insight for leaders. While our future scenario will have a systemic, evolving characteristic to it, it is not without unexpected syntheses, things we could not predict from response to needs. Finally, how this new vision is defined will make a difference on whether we will ever be able to lead anyone there! It is terribly difficult to make microlevel predictions on the nature of the future, but our ability to understand macrolevel forces will help us navigate the present and direct people into the future. For leaders, and as leaders, applied sociologists can empower themselves and others to take charge of their own futures.

Other sociological tools are essential. We have already demonstrated the importance of taking the high ground—the macro perspective—if one is a leader. Sociologists in general, and applied sociologists specifically, are trained to see the world this way. We have a vantage point to see the big picture as well as to look into the future. Our basic research methods training is crucial to engaging leadership problems in a systematic, data-driven manner. To say that leadership is one applied problem after another would not stretch the truth! Creating and/or accessing and then using valid information is essential for decision making. Often, determining what is valid information and locating sources for it can be important to leaders. Critical here is a solid understanding of theory's association with methods and a willingness to investigate new theoretical positions. In addition, knowledge of organizations, on one level, and demographics (i.e., human population), on another level, is valuable. Maintaining this perspective helps us think globally and act locally. Some of the elements of social psychology are extremely valuable in translating the macro perspective to those who will follow. Understanding of small groups, attitudes, and public opinion are just some of the tools that come with the sociological package.

Finally, and perhaps most importantly, the sociological imagination can be a tool for leading. Once we have viewed the world from a macro view, we need to take this view and translate it into creative outcomes that frame the present and the future. Understanding how things could be, given the proper social conditions, is essential for leaders. Sociologists deal with ambiguity. In fact, they are comfortable with it. Creating a dynamic, changing vision for the future should be a common tool for sociologists.

▧ Presentation Tools

Making presentations on leadership has many elements and, hence, is challenging. We have made a case that leadership is anchored in the present, past, and future. People often have trouble with any one of these states of being, let alone all of them. Maybe this could best be demonstrated by modeling, moraling, and molding.

One of the most difficult perspectives to present is the important connection to the future that leaders need to provide. In short, you are asking people to go somewhere that, for all practical purposes, does not exist! Therefore, we must create a meaningful fabrication in which we can reasonably imagine conducting our lives. One of the ways to construct this world is through the construction of scenes that might exist in the future: scenarios. People are unlikely to follow if there is no plausible path to where you are going! We need a clear path to follow. Pictures can be extremely valuable in setting people on this path.

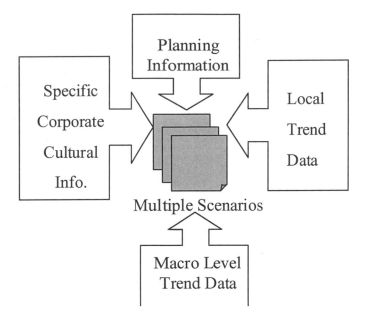

Figure 5.1 Some Forces Shaping Scenarios

It is a great deal easier to lead people somewhere if you know where you are going! Scenarios make this possible because they make the future concrete. We must be able to get our hands on the future. How will we do this? Later in this book, we will examine change and trend analysis. Both of these will be useful. We can build the scenarios ourselves. We can have our clients build them, or we can work in tandem with clients to do this. Let us take some steps to a scenario (see Figure 5.1).

First, we need to scan the environment to get a sense of the forces that are affecting the present and future. Clients may have data that give us a sense of this, but you may need to collect this information. Population data, local or state planning data, and published reports on the future can be valuable here. Assembling this information is not enough. Put yourself in the role of the client. Imagine having 20 pounds of reports dropped on your desk with a comment such as, "Hi, read this. We will be writing scenarios next week!" Impossible! So, second, you will probably need to extract the key information for them. This may take the form of an annotated list of central factors influencing the future, with an accompanying transparency to put on an overhead projector.

Third, get your clients to pay attention to the list! This is difficult. People are busy, and scenario writing is not at the top of their to-do list! For some groups, distributing the information in advance would be helpful, but it may end up in the recycling bin. This means that you will need to distribute and discuss your list at your scenario-writing session. A graphic presentation of the forces acting on the situation could be a valuable tool for your presentation.

Fourth, when scenario-writing day comes, you must be prepared to present the global forces from your environmental scan (external forces), extract and identify the local forces within the organization (internal), and clearly state the condition that is the focus of your scenario. Now, you are ready to discuss how things are in the present. This can be graphic, relative to the problem: "What happens on an average day now?" A flip chart or an overhead with a transparency and grease pencil can be useful for noting the current state of affairs.

But you need to move into the future (your fifth step). It may be helpful to recommend a specific target for the future. This is relative to the problem itself. Many human events unfold in a number of days. Technology transfer may unfold in weeks, months, or years; major cultural change may unfold in decades. It is difficult for most people to think in the future, so, when in doubt, pin down a point in the relatively near future, such as 3 to 5 years. Be specific. Is it 3 or 5? For example, say, "Let us consider the social forces we have discussed and our outline of the present, and then think about things in 5 years." (If 1997, say in the year 2002.)

Now, moving to our sixth step, we want to brainstorm for the future. This can be done in many ways, but one useful way is to actually "take" people to the future! This can be expressed cognitively or in behavior. Here are two examples: For this problem, let us consider the manner by which higher education is delivered in the year 2002.

- (Cognitive) "Close your eyes for a moment and relax. Reflect on the forces we have been discussing. Now, imagine this is December 10, 2002. How are people learning in what we currently call higher education today?"
- (Behavior) "It is December 10, 2002. You are engaged in the learning process in a higher education system. Role-play the things that you will be doing today. Write a story about what you did today."

Record the responses to these. If you are responsible for the scenario, the outline will be the ingredients that you can write into the scenario. You might want to videotape the role plays. Asking people to write is useful on two fronts. First, writing stimulates thought (behavior-cognition), and second, you can collect the scenarios as "data." Regardless, you will need to move to the seventh step.

Now, you need to integrate these ideas into a written or graphic picture of this scene in the year 2002. This may be done overnight (you may lose your clients), or better yet, on the spot. You can shape this as an outline; a paragraph (a computer, word processor, and projection system would be great, but flip charts work); or a picture.

Your eighth step is to get feedback on the scenario. Does it feel right to those in the room? Can we get consensus on the picture? Here, we are looking for a collective definition of reality or realities. Understand that there may be two or more pictures. Make changes as necessary to each picture. You may need to restate the entire scene, redraw the pictures, or rewrite the paragraphs. As a ninth step, you may want to circulate scenario(s) for feedback after your meeting. Allow some time for people to reflect on what they have done.

The tenth step is to "report out" the scenario(s) to your clients. This may be a written report, a formal presentation, and/or a computerized presentation. Regardless, be prepared for more input. This is an iterative process. Keep going until (a) there are no more changes, (b) your client tells you to stop, or (c) the contract runs out!

Sociologist as Expert

Whether it is moraling, modeling, or molding, sociologists have the perspectives and tools to be leaders, or at the very least, to assist others to lead. Applied sociologists have a sense of the nature of collective beliefs, values, and norms. They know how these elements are the backbones of structure and, hence, how they guide human action.

Additionally, application of microlevel sociological principles is useful in the development of leaders. Leaders can take the role of leader, demonstrate the role, and export the role to others. We know the value of modeling leadership characteristics. We also know the vulnerabilities of humans. To this extent, sociological traditions to protect the rights of human subjects are essential. And, finally, sociologists hold to the notion that most human patterns can be learned. Sociologists are very likely to believe that leaders are made, not born. Hence, we can create leaders. Applied sociologists can locate and recommend structures within society for the production of leaders.

⅗ Case Study

A national professional organization was facing problems. After operating for more than 10 years, it found itself unable to grow. It seemed to be going nowhere. Reaching a membership high of just over 1,500 members, in the past 3 years it has been unable to return to that membership level, with membership rarely increasing above 1,000. Membership turnover rates reflect that the organization has trouble keeping members for an extended period of time. The administrative officer has just resigned, citing the organization's inability to provide and fulfill an adequate benefits package to its members. The organization elects its president, vice president, and secretary for 1-year terms. Board members serve for 3-year terms. Organization products, as well as the newsletter and other major publications, are erratic in delivery. The annual meeting of the group is excellent, but the euphoria of the group rapidly deteriorates into inactivity. Finances based largely on membership dues are shaky.

The board of directors has hired you to evaluate the organization's situation, specifically assessing the organization's leadership problems. Your task is to use the characteristics of leadership that you have learned in this chapter and the tools provided in other chapters to provide a solution to these problems.

Possible Solution

Here are some ways to think of a solution to this problem. Analyzing this problem and coming up with solutions draws on much of the preceding chapters. We will focus largely on leadership, but we will also draw from the material on process and structure. Listed below are a number of possible approaches that we may take to solve this problem. Let us take each separately:

Leaders Have a Clear Vision of the Future

Organizations and individuals need to have a vision of their future. They need to have a direction in which to travel in order to commit resources effectively. Leaders of this organization also need a sense of direction. They need to have a part in defining the vision and have consensus in it. The following is what you might recommend.

Recommend that the board of directors conduct a meeting or retreat to reflect on the organization's vision. It will be critical to meet with key stakeholders prior to the meeting or retreat. Before the meeting or retreat, do the following:

1. Make certain that the president, key board members, and other stakeholders have a vision! You cannot assume this to be the case.
2. Tracing the corporate vision will require that you locate the formal and informal leaders and power brokers in the organization. Weber's work is helpful here. Of course, you will look for the "legalistic" leaders, the ones who have been elected or promoted to positions of authority. But you will also need to find the "traditional" and the "charismatic" leaders. Traditional leaders are the ones who have arisen in the corporate culture. They may hold formal office, or they may not! They may be obvious to you, or they may not be apparent on the surface. Consult some of the organization's senior members to find these important people. The charismatic leaders have attracted a following in their own right. These people often have a good personal sense of vision themselves and attract others to them.
3. Review the organization's documents regarding vision. You will need to request copies of current and past strategic plans, as well as formal and informal survey research of the corporation and its clients. If no formal documents are available, interview key informants as to their informal perception of the vision for the organization.
   a. Analyze the content of these documents. What do they suggest the corporate vision should be?
   b. How does this vision contrast with the informal vision you have gathered from the stakeholders?
4. Prepare a brief assessment in writing of what the corporate vision appears to be. This will likely appear as one of the following:
   a. A dominant single vision with consensus
   b. A pronounced vision, but no consensus or support
   c. Multiple visions, each different and with little consensus for the organization as a whole
   d. No vision at all

To enhance the board's ability to lead, your goal is to clarify the vision. Your task in holding the meeting or retreat will be altered by your findings in Part 4c above. If you discover that single or multiple visions exist, with or without consensus, your task in the meeting or retreat will be to clarify a single vision and find consensus. If, however, no vision exists, you may need to change the focus of the meeting or

retreat to a focus group assessing needs. You may even wish to post-
pone the meeting or retreat until you have been able to clarify needs
and/or have conducted an environmental scan. Review Chapter 2. Refresh your memory on the items related to strategic planning.

Leaders Provide Structure in the Midst of Chaos and Change

Once the board has reached a collective vision that has general
commitment by the organization's membership, organizational planning must follow.

1. With the organization's leaders, organize a procedure for the development of a strategic plan for the organization.
2. Use the planning elements outlined in Chapter 2 as your goals for this
   planning procedure. To refresh your memory, these elements were the
   following:
   a. Do an environmental scan (take a reading of the social factors that
      surround us and determine just how they relate to the plan we are
      about to write).
   b. Revisit the vision.
   c. A vision is necessary to direct just where it is we are planning to go.
      Construct a mission statement. Just what is our purpose for creating
      this structure?
   d. What is our mission?
   e. What are the organization's goals?
   f. What are the organization's objectives?
   g. Develop a strategy for evaluating the plan.
3. Planning is a dynamic, ongoing process that is not completed in a day. Be
   prepared to spend time and energy in developing the plan and getting
   consensus on it. The stakeholders must "own" the plan in order for it to
   work.

Leaders Can Mobilize Others to Commit

Formulating a plan does not mean that it will be enacted. A plan
must be "sold" to all those who are guided by it. Leaders must gain
commitment from customers inside and outside the organization.

1. Put the plan in operation.
   a. Develop a clear set of actions and accompanying budget to enact the
      plan.
   b. Guide organizational leaders toward assigning responsibility and re-
      sources for completing the actions.

c. Set up realistic mechanisms for determining if the actions were completed (monitoring), and evaluate the impact of the actions (summative evaluation).

d. Create procedures to determine how the plan may change to improve performance (formative evaluation).

2. Simultaneously sell the plan to those who must follow it.

a. Hold training sessions to clarify the organization's mission.

b. Provide newsletter stories and personal presentations describing the vision, mission, and goals.

c. Clarify and circulate the vision and mission. Make them available on all corporate material.

d. Market the vision inside and outside the organization.

▧ Exercises

1. Use Ackoff's model for planning for the future described in this chapter. Focus on a trend or some social situation occurring in your area. Now, write four different scenarios, one each for reactive, inactive, preactive, and proactive perspectives; outline how each situation might change in the next 3 years and then in the next 5 years. Describe how a leader might need to respond differently to each scenario.

2. In this work, we contend that leaders are made, not born. If this is the case, we should be able to identify social structures that have been created to produce leaders. Make a leadership inventory in your area (target a town, city, county, state, etc.). Methodically review the business, government, religious, educational, community, and familial categories of leadership available. List as many organizations as possible. For each, determine the target audience (children, early teen, later teen, young adult, and adult). Write or discuss the nature of the groups currently engaged in an effort to create leaders.

3. Construct a personal leadership inventory for yourself. List some of the characteristics of leadership outlined in this chapter. Then, for each, determine the extent to which you are "not at all like this," "somewhat like this," or "very much like this." For areas in which you are "not at all" or "somewhat" like the dimension you have listed, write a plan to improve that characteristic. Whether you act on this or not, you will have the beginning profile of a course for your future.

Maneuvering the Multicultural Minefield

☙ Living in an Ever-Changing World

As sociologists, we are living during a very exciting time in history. Every day, something new is happening in our world. Who would have expected, in our lifetimes, that the USSR would crumble and the Eastern European countries would gain their independence with as little bloodshed as they did? As you read your paper today or watch the world news tonight, you will be observing dramatic political and social changes that were unthinkable even a decade ago.

As the 21st century approaches, we really do live in a global community. Events happening in remote corners of the world affect us in this country almost as soon as they happen. Do you remember the Gulf War? Iraq attacked Kuwait and was countered by a force of soldiers from a number of countries, including the United States. Your neighbor, or possibly even a family member, was in the National Guard. All of a sudden, his or her unit was called up for active duty and sent to the Persian Gulf. Do you remember the hardships, the change of plans, and the disruption of family life? Let us bring it even closer to you. As the Iraqis were retreating from Kuwait, they burned oil field after oil field. This caused a depletion in the amount of oil available for use around the world. Because your car runs on gasoline, you pull up to the pump to find that the prices have risen dramatically. You grudgingly pay the additional costs and wonder how much higher they will go. Thus, you have been directly affected by a series of events that happened halfway around the world.

Instantaneous global communication has made us all aware of other cultures and has forced us to become knowledgeable of how these cultures are different from our own. You can literally call, fax, or e-mail anyone anywhere in the world within minutes. Communication satellites allow us to view events happening in real time. Do you remember CNN correspondents reporting from Baghdad while the allies were bombing the city? For the first time in history, you could watch a battle "live," but from the vantage point of the other side. Communication innovations, such as the Internet, are opening up doors and additional information sources that were not even thought of a couple of decades ago. When the authors were children, the television was a new invention. The screen was less than 12 inches, the picture was in black and white, and the reception was fuzzy. You were lucky if you could pick up three or four channels. Today, televisions are not only in color, they are also in stereo, on cable, and in many cases, you can tune in to anywhere from 50 to 500 different stations.

With the growth of the global communications phenomenon came the rapid growth of global markets. In the late 20th century, it has become very hard for a country or culture to isolate itself from others. U.S. companies are looking for markets around the world in which they can sell their products and services. At the same time, foreign companies are viewing the affluent U.S. market as a very fruitful environment to grow their product lines and profits. As these companies enter new cultures, they very quickly find out that "doing things the way we used to" no longer holds true.

Different cultures have different normative and belief systems. People act and do things in ways that we might originally find strange, and we may actually be uncomfortable with these cultural differences. Businesses, highly successful in selling their products in the United States, may find it very difficult to attract new customers in cultures where their products make little or no sense. For example, most Americans live in fairly large houses or apartments. We tend to buy big, that is, big cars, big furniture, and big appliances. We have also been taught to buy food in bulk sizes to save money. However, most cultures around the world live small. That is, families live in small houses or apartments. They may own a car, but it is usually small and fuel efficient. They may also have appliances, such as refrigerators, but these items are usually less than half the size of ours. In most cultures, it is quite common for a family member to purchase fresh bread, meat, and produce in the morning at a local market for the family to consume during that day. Think what it would be like if you had to do this every day. However, it is a part of their culture and is not viewed as the inconvenience it would be here.

Even within the United States, the understanding of cultural and ethnic differences has become essential. When we were in high school, it was common for us to hear that the United States was a cultural melting pot. That is, the best ideas, values, and attitudes from each culture are mixed into one amalgamated blend that we call America. Recently, the analogy has changed from the melting pot to the "stew pot." Each culture adds its unique flavor to the American blend. Like a good stew, however, each cultural ingredient maintains its own identity. To a person from outside the United States, we are all considered Americans; but among each other, we are very conscious of our ethnic backgrounds and heritage.

Throughout the 1980s and 1990s, major population growth in the United States has been among ethnic populations. Demographic projections indicate that white population growth during the next 10 years will continue to remain relatively flat. Growth will be with the African American, Hispanic, and Asian segments of the population, with the Hispanic population projected to grow the fastest.

With the increased growth in population also comes an increase in social and economic power. Ethnic populations will continue to grow politically and, at the same time, wield more economic power. As this power is converted into action, it is even more imperative that we understand the nuances in attitudinal, behavioral, and cultural differences in each of the ethnic groups. For example, it may be incorrect to view an ethnic group, such as Hispanics, as one group. Mexican culture differs from other Central and South American cultures, which differ from a Puerto Rican culture, which is different from a Cuban one. Similarly, there is no one Asian or European culture. As the ethnic groups differ from the dominant culture on a macroscopic level, so then do they differ from each other on the microscopic level.

This diversity will continue to grow and manifest itself into the next millennium. As social scientists, the challenge we face is when to emphasize the cultural stew and when to emphasize the individual ingredients. When we do emphasize one area over the other, what effect will that area have on others in the culture? To successfully compete in the 21st century, a good understanding of each group's unique cultural heritage, values, and customs, coupled with the knowledge of how and when the diversity fits in other cultures, is a necessity.

▧ The Multicultural Minefield

Although the global arena is full of opportunities, it is also full of pitfalls and, in some cases, land mines. Understanding different cultures is a learned behavior that is constantly being redefined and adapted as the individual cultures and the interaction between them changes. Although many cultures have fairly routinized patterns of behavior, these behaviors may be interpreted somewhat differently within the culture. For example, individuals living in Paris speak and act differently from their fellow citizens living in the rest of France, and people living in northern France have different traditions from those living in the south. Thus, not all French are the same, and saying or doing something in one area may be viewed as inappropriate and offensive in another.

With the recent division of many Eastern European countries into smaller ethnic regions, the multicultural minefield has taken on a very real portrayal. Ancient tribal differences have resurfaced, and ancient hatreds have been rekindled. Not only is it wrong to say or do something wrong in these areas, it is downright dangerous. As an expert in cultural diversity, you will have to understand the history of these differences and which current social conditions are causing the divisiveness today. At the same time, you will have to demonstrate objectivity in dealing with all groups or your credibility will be called into question by one side or the other.

On the macro scale, the same situation holds true. It is inaccurate to talk about "Europe" without underscoring the socioeconomic and cultural differences. Western Europe is demographically and culturally different from Eastern Europe. Western European economies tend to be older and more stable. Eastern European economies, on the other hand, are in the midst of a dramatic transformation from state-based to free-market economies. Families in the West tend to be older, and the standard of living is quite good. On the other hand, Eastern European unemployment is high, and the families are young. These two factors, by themselves, may actually effect changes in the cultures of Western Europe. Young eastern families are migrating west in search of employment. As they move, they will bring their cultural attitudes and behaviors with them. Many of these cultural differences will be internalized gradually into their new cultures. This is nothing new when one remembers the early days of the United States and how different attitudes, behaviors, and vocabularies blended together over the years to form the culture we have today.

Cultural diversity and dynamic multiculturalism are evident around the globe. There is really no such person as an "Asian," because that region of the world consists of a number of diverse cultures, languages, and religions. Indians differ from the Chinese, who differ from the Japanese, who differ from Koreans, who differ from Malaysians and Indonesians. Within each of these dominant cultures, the differences are further compounded by whether you live in a metropolitan or rural area. Most metropolitan areas have populations that range in the millions. These city-states tend to be more modern and more adaptable to outside influences than do their rural counterparts.

Even within the United States, regional, ethnic, and cultural differences make it difficult for us to talk about an "American" culture. Sure, there are many things that we share across the United States, and we are pretty similar in the ways that we do things. But these similarities have their own unique twists as we move to different parts of the country. People living in the North tend to view the world somewhat differently than do those in the South. Similarly, one's attitudes and behaviors differ if you live in the Northeast as compared to the Southwest. Although we all speak a common language, American English, our use of the language (dialects, accents, idioms, slang) differs based on the part of the country in which we live.

Thus, understanding cultural diversity is not as simple as it sounds. Even within cultures, there are little nuances or differences that make it hard for the cultural analyst to be 100% accurate in his or her interpretation of the culture. However, the multicultural minefield can be mapped if the analyst is aware of the possibility of these differences and is objective in his or her approach to identifying and interpreting them. The cultural analyst must be able to place the culture and its unique attributes into its own social milieu or situation. Although it is essential that the analyst look at the differences between cultures, he or she must not subjectively judge one culture to be better or worse than another. The successful cultural analyst is sensitive to these differences and attempts to find out why these behaviors and attitudes fit the social situation in which they are found.

▧ Why Understand Cultural Differences?

The problem of understanding and adapting to cultural differences affects each one of us at a number of different levels. At the microscopic or personal level, understanding cultural differences allows you to change personal attitudes and perceptions. You have the ability to break down some of the old stereotypes or misconceptions you had developed about different cultures or ethnic groups. You will learn to understand why people do things differently and how some of the ways they do things may actually make your life easier. You also may find out that many of the differences in behavior that you originally observed may not be all that different from what you are used to doing.

Being able to understand cultural differences will actually broaden your personal boundaries. Individuals who can understand differences and, more importantly, find ways to maximize the effectiveness of those cultural differences will be a highly sought-after resource by businesses and government in the next decade. It will not be enough to be able to speak a foreign language (although this is a basic necessity); individuals will have to be able to understand different cultures and then interpret the data in such a way that policies and decisions can be made effectively. Not only will this skill that you developed allow you to work with others better, it will give you opportunities for new and exciting assignments around the world.

Many companies today are actively looking for "global analysts." These individuals must be able to identify and understand cultural differences and trends. Trends can run the gamut from large-scale global trends, such as the economy, to very small localized trends, such as the use of automated teller machines in Cairo. The global analyst must be able to find information on the country or culture and must be able to present it in such a way that his or her audience can understand and use it. This usually means taking the data and showing the differences between our culture and the culture under study. However, the good analyst takes this process at least one step further. The analyst shows why the differences exist and why they are important to the culture. At the same time, the analyst shows how the client can use these differences to best market his or her products or services.

Obviously, having these skills will increase your job opportunities. Not only will you be in demand here in the United States, but other groups from outside of the United States will be looking for individuals who can help them understand those little confusing differences and nuances that are prevalent in the American society. You will then be able to use your skills and expertise in a unique way. You will have to explain American culture as it is viewed by another culture. For example, if your employer is from Japan, your explanation of the way things are done in the United States will have to be in terms and ideas that your Japanese audience will understand.

All of this leads to the macroscopic or large-scale level. Innovations in communications and technology will make the global community exactly that. It will become more and more a community in which ideas and, it is hoped, solutions will be shared instantaneously from one culture to another. People living in the global community will be the most informed individuals in history. Information, however, is subject to interpretation and misinterpretation. Therefore, it will be essential for citizens of the global community to identify and interpret cultural differences and understand how they are intertwined and integrated.

⚂ Cultural Concepts

There are a number of sociological concepts that are very important for the understanding of cultures and cultural differences. First of all, when we talk about culture, we are talking about all of the material (tools, products, clothes, etc.) and nonmaterial (ideas, attitudes, etc.) factors that go together to give this group its unique identity. It is as important to understand the way the culture works and plays as it is to understand how it thinks. Make sure that when you are analyzing a culture, you look at the material and nonmaterial aspects across all segments of that culture. Often, the magazines and television will portray the more glitzy, "high-culture" aspects of a society. However, this lifestyle may affect only a small portion of individuals in that culture. It is more important to find out and understand how the overwhelming majority of the culture lives, thinks, and acts.

Another extremely important concept to understand when you are dealing with cultural diversity and multiculturalism is *ethnocentrism*. In a nutshell, this concept focuses on the idea that one's own group or culture is better than all others. Although this concept may serve its purpose when you are talking about loyalty to your school or sports teams, it is a biasing factor when you are looking at behaviors and attitudes that are different from yours. If you try to judge other cultures solely on how you feel about your own, you will inevitably find the other culture wanting or not meeting your standards. In reality, the differences that you find unique are really a way of life in other cultures. On the other hand, if members of that culture were to look at your culture, we are sure that many things you say or do would be questionable and, in some cases, offensive to them.

Instead of taking an ethnocentric approach, the sociologist must be culturally sensitive and attempt to understand the attitudes and behaviors relative to a culture's own unique set of circumstances. This allows you to better understand why things are done the way they are in that culture and allows you to quickly and accurately identify the norms and patterns of behavior expected in the culture. This does not mean that you cannot disagree with the way things are done in the culture under investigation. No culture is perfect, and just because something is culturally acceptable does not necessarily mean that it is correct. However, it is extremely important to understand how that idea or activity came into being and how powerfully it is intertwined with other aspects of the culture.

Another sociological concept related to this is the notion of "taking the role of the other." When you are observing another culture, it is important to get a feeling for how people in that culture think. One of the best ways to do this is to try to view the culture from the eyes of one who is a part of the culture. As you learn more about a culture, constantly play out the role of being a member of it. How would you respond to the ways things are done, the ways people think, their political and social attitudes, and so on? Remember, you are playing the role of a member of the culture and cannot think in your normal cultural terms. The first couple of times you do this role playing, it is hard because you cannot separate your existing attitudes from the role you are playing. After you have gained more information on the culture and more experience in the role-playing process, you will find the task to be very thought provoking and actually a fun thing to do.

Finally, as a sociologist, you need to use a number of theoretical perspectives to analyze a culture. Using a symbolic interaction perspective, you will want to ascertain what the various material and nonmaterial components of a culture mean to the individuals who are a part of it. Keep in mind that there will not be one answer to this analysis. Different individuals and groups within the culture will place different meanings on the actions and artifacts in the culture. As a structuralist, you will want to develop an understanding of the key social institutions and how they interrelate with each other. You will want to look at how the organizations function to maintain the culture. Finally, you will want to use a conflict approach to understand the inequities and inconsistencies that exist. For example, how are different ethnic groups and minorities treated in the culture? How are the members of the society stratified? What types of interaction exist between the social classes? These questions and others like them will help you to define the real culture as opposed to the ideal culture that may be portrayed in the media or by the ruling body or government.

Investigating another culture calls for a combination of the above perspectives. Using one perspective by itself will prove to be quite limiting and will give you only a piece of the information. On the other hand, using a combination of perspectives will allow you to gain a number of views on how the culture works or does not work. This will define the culture more accurately and will give you a more realistic view of this highly dynamic entity.

Research Tools

There are a number of research tools you can use to learn about other cultures. These tools usually run the gamut from simple observation to full-scale multicultural surveys. Each will give you valuable information and insights. By themselves, however, each technique is limited and will offer only pieces of the overall picture. For this reason, we highly recommend that you triangulate with a number of tools in order to obtain a more detailed and accurate view of the culture.

At the simplest level is observation. Although this technique will not yield a database of hard, scientific facts on a culture, it is very important in helping you develop your baseline perspective about the culture. Attend cultural events, restaurants, and church services. Visit with members of that culture and ask them for their perspective on the culture. A number of colleges are currently offering "cultural immersion" programs. These programs are oriented toward giving the participant a basic understanding of a culture in a short period of time. Many programs are a day or two in duration and include such things as attending lectures and cultural events, interactive discussions with individuals from the culture, and spending time with families from the culture.

Most universities also offer programs in which you can study abroad for a semester or a year.

While you are going through the observation process, you should also begin to develop a database on the culture. This secondary analysis technique is quite helpful and, in the age of the information superhighway, is relatively inexpensive. Most libraries and bookstores carry a wide variety of information on countries and cultures. These materials are usually in the form of travel books, maps, and videotapes.

Having access to the Internet will also open many avenues of information. There are numerous profiles on countries ranging from KGB/CIA country analyses to various U.S. government bureau and departmental reports. Likewise, most countries are now advertising themselves on the Internet, and summaries of key newspapers usually can be found.

At the more macroscopic level, numerous international research firms have completed large multinational surveys of various cultures and consumers. These reports are sometimes made available for a nominal fee (especially to students), but they can also become very expensive, ranging in the thousands of dollars.

The above tools represent only a few examples of ways in which you can obtain data and information on a given culture. There are many others available, and, just as important, any of the above can be adapted to meet your unique needs. Again, the best way to gain an understanding is to triangulate using a number of techniques and develop a comprehensive database. Keep in mind, however, that cultures are dynamic, and changes occur. Therefore, the database must be reviewed and updated on an ongoing basis.

⊠ Presentation Tools

Having a storehouse of information available does you no good if you do not have a way to present it meaningfully to a variety of audiences. Because your audiences will have different reasons for needing the information, you will need to interpret and present the information at different levels. Remember that culture exists at a number of different levels. Not only do you need to understand the culture you are researching but also the culture or cultures receiving the presentation. These presentations can range from a report to a full-blown presentation.

If you are writing a report, remember that your audience will most likely have preconceived notions about the culture that you have investigated. It is wise to have a very good understanding of what the audience understands about the culture and what they expect from your analysis. You should make sure that your report is concise and directly addresses their concerns. Our experience is that the use of photographs and cultural artifacts helps to give the reader a better mental picture of what you are talking about.

If you have to make a formal presentation, focus on the key learnings you have obtained from your study. Although you may be very interested in minute details, your audience will most likely want overall results. Remember, you can always give them the details later. Good presentations, especially ones on understanding cultural differences, require the use of visuals and other artifacts that help give the members of the audience something tangible on which to focus. This could be in the form of attire, products, pictures, graphics, and even the refreshments served.

It is also very important that you serve as the interface between the audience and the culture. You will be asked why cultures do things in certain ways. Not only will you be expected to interpret this into concepts or activities that the audience will understand, you will have to explain why these behaviors differ from ours and why they fit the culture in which they are situated. In this case, you are actually taking on the role of a member of that culture.

Finally, although you will know more about the culture than your audience does, leave yourself open to gain new information and understandings about the culture. You may be asked a question during the presentation that gives you another perspective from which to view the culture. Use this perspective as another way to triangulate your interpretation of the data and your understanding of the culture.

▧ Sociologist as Expert

As a sociologist, you have unique training and skills that will enable you to become a successful cultural analyst. You have learned to take a systematic approach to analyzing issues and problems. You have learned to look at a situation from different perspectives and to try to understand how others are viewing the situation. Most importantly, you have learned to take an objective view of different ideas, attitudes, and behaviors. Although you may not personally agree with some of these cultural differences, you have learned to step into a professional role and attempt to understand how and why these differences occur in another culture.

As a researcher, you have a knowledge of the tools available (or where to get them) to successfully analyze a culture or cultures. You know which tools are appropriate for given situations and which tools will provide the most meaningful results. Because you know that each tool has its limitations, you know that you must use a combination of them to understand the culture more fully.

Finally, as the analyst, you are the key for others to understand the culture. Your training enables you to present a thorough analysis of the culture and present your results in such a way that a number of audiences will understand them. Most importantly, you are able to take on the role of the other (whether it is another culture or diverse groups or audiences) and make your analysis meaningful and *actionable* for all groups involved. This is where the "expert" title really begins to fit.

Case Study

The Case

A *Fortune* 500 company has hired you to develop a cultural awareness and training program for their employees. The company wants all of their people to have a basic understanding of cultural diversity and wants employees to be sensitive to ethnic and cultural differences when dealing with their customers. Because the company plans to double its sales outside of North America over the next 5 years, management feels that it is essential for the employees to say and do the right things as they develop and grow a multicultural customer base.

Your task is to create a program that will open the employees' eyes to cultural differences. This program must be designed to meet the needs of everyone in the company, from the janitor to the CEO. Remember, different individuals will have different levels of awareness and expertise in this area. At the same time, each individual will have his or her own unique motivations for wanting to participate in the program.

The company has given you a very limited budget and has asked you to use the resources already available in the company or community. How would you handle this project?

Possible Solutions

Following are a number of possible solutions to the problem. Keep in mind that no one technique will handle all of your needs, and in all likelihood, you will want to use a combination of the techniques in your program.

Identification

Employees need to be familiar with the key cultures and geographical areas in which the company does business. You would be surprised by the large number of people who do not know where countries are located.

1. In the lobby or another central location, have the company place flags for each of the countries in which it does business.
2. Put a series of clocks on the wall to show the different time zones for each of the countries.
3. Place world maps in strategic locations around the building showing the geographical relationship of the areas to the company's headquarters and other facilities.
4. Prepare brief (no more than three pages) factbooks on the country. These factbooks should include social, political, demographic, and cultural information, among other things.
5. Use international employees and available community resources to develop an on-site international fair. This fair should include areas or booths in which cultural information about the country or ethnic group is presented. The fair should include cultural artifacts, customs, dress, food, and some small handout that the employee can take home.

Training

Once the employees have begun to develop an awareness of other cultures, you can move to the training stage. The training stage can run from simple communication etiquette to formal language training.

1. Develop a short manual and training session on how to place and receive telephone calls and written correspondence in different cultures.

2. Develop a short course (1 to 2 hours) on proper business and social etiquette in other cultures.
3. Create a half-day workshop on the culture under investigation. This should include an expert coming in to talk about the culture and a project in which the participants attempt to solve a problem or market question related to that area.
4. Use community resources (international agencies, universities) to develop a series of cultural immersion programs.
5. Have the company contract with the local university(s) to develop a special in-house series of language courses.

Resources

Once employees are trained, they will naturally want more information on the cultures they have just learned about. The best way to handle this is to have the company set up an international resource center. This resource center should contain both physical (library) and electronic (on-line database) components. Included in these components should be the following:

1. Books, magazines, videotapes, maps, and newspapers from the culture
2. Easily accessible profiles of the country or culture
3. A database of internal company information about the culture, such as trip reports that people make when they visit that culture
4. A link to on-line databases (Internet, National Trade Data Bank, etc.) that will allow the user the ability to do searches for additional information on the country or culture
5. A computer setup that allows for a global information network that lets the company link all of its offices and facilities together to share information. Many times, this is the easiest way to get information on a culture, and the employee has the added advantage of hearing the information firsthand from someone participating in that culture.

The above are just a small number of techniques that have been used to develop multicultural awareness and sensitivity. As the cultural expert, you should choose from this list or other techniques to develop the best program to meet your client's needs. Remember that in most cases, you will have a number of different audiences and that the techniques must be tailored to each of these groups. Above all, remember to be creative and to make the program an enjoyable learning exercise.

▧ Exercises

There are a number of simple exercises you can do to help you better understand cultural diversity. The following exercises can be used to study differences across cultures as well as cultural variations within a particular country. These exercises require some basic library or on-line research and a lot of observation. Thinking about how cultural differences affect you should become part of your normal daily activity.

1. As you read the paper or watch the world news, make a list of cultural behaviors or attitudes that are new and interesting to you. Make it a personal project to find out why these cultural events occur in that culture and what purposes they serve. Next, ask yourself if something similar exists in your culture. If it does, what are the similarities and the differences? If it does not, what do you think would happen if it was introduced into your culture?

2. Make it a hobby or pet project to immerse yourself in other cultures. Attend cultural exhibits, read books and articles, go to restaurants, and attend other events that are put on by members of that culture. Introduce yourself to members of the culture and learn from them. (People like to talk about themselves and the ways in which they do things.) Try to gain an understanding of why people think, act, and live the way they do.

3. If you have the opportunity to visit another culture, put on your research thinking cap. Visit stores and restaurants. Watch television, look at local magazines and newspapers, and see what the current trends and interests are. Visit with people, especially in their homes, and see what is normal behavior in their culture.

4. This exercise is the most fun but also probably the hardest to do. Take one day in your life and analyze everything you do from the perspective of someone totally unfamiliar with your culture. Ask yourself how someone else would interpret what and how you eat, how you act going to or from work or school, the way you interact with family members and others, and the activities you do for fun and entertainment. Try to be as objective as possible. Remember, you are in the role

of an outsider looking at behaviors about which you do not normally spend much time thinking. In some cases, you may begin to wonder about some of the things you say or do.

Understanding and Organizing Change

☒ Adapting to an Ever-Changing World

Each one of us wakes every morning to a world that has changed dramatically from the previous day. As an applied sociologist, these changes should pique your curiosity and make you want to understand them better. You will want to know how these changes affect the attitudes and behaviors of those around you. Most importantly, you will want to understand how these changes influence the way you think and act.

One of the first things you will want to do is identify the change. Is the change large (macroscopic) or small (microscopic)? Does it affect a small number of people or whole cultures and societies? Is the change easily adaptable to normal day-to-day living, or will it disrupt the familiar and the comfortable? By asking these questions, you are beginning to place the change into a social context. By isolating the social context, you gain the ability to place meaning around the change. This is where the sociologist really begins to have fun.

Change means many different things to individuals, groups, and cultures. Actually, individuals within the same group or culture may view it differently based on their own unique backgrounds, experiences, and socialization. This is why studying human behavior can become so complex, but at the same time, so interesting. Two people viewing change differently will generate different responses. These responses, coupled with the reactions that the individuals have to each other's responses, will in all likelihood cause additional change.

Understanding change means being able to identify trends and project their future direction. But this may not be as easy as it sounds. The trajectory that change takes is not always a simple straight line. Change may be obvious, such as a new job, or it may be more subtle, such as an economy slowly moving toward a recession. It may be layered, in that a whole series of other changes are set in place by one seemingly simple change. Finally, the way in which groups define the change may lead to a whole new set of behaviors, some of which may be predictable.

As applied sociologists, we are as much interested in the effects of the change as we are with the change itself. What are the consequences brought on by the change? How are different individuals, groups, and cultures affected by the change? How do they define and respond to it? What happens if two different groups respond to the change in totally different ways? What happens if the individuals affected by the change view the results as being uncomfortable or even painful? These are all questions you will want to examine as you investigate a change event or series of events.

Probably one of the best change indicators used by the media and business world today is that of trends. The process of identifying and tracking trends has actually become a business unto itself. Some individuals make millions of dollars annually by telling others that they have the unique ability to identify, interpret, and predict new trends that affect business and society. Whether they are accurate or not is a subject for another conversation. What is important here is the amount of importance placed on understanding and responding to these indicators of change.

⚜ Understanding Trends

"The American population is aging," "Individuals are afraid of being victims of a crime," and "Anyone can speak to anyone else in the world in a matter of seconds." These are all examples of trends that affect each one of us. We are all getting older, so this is not a great revelation in and of itself. But when the trend is placed in a social context, it offers up many more meanings. The fact that we are aging has implications at both a microscopic and macroscopic level. At the microscopic level, as we age, our lifestyles change. These changes will evoke other changes, such as how we look at others, how others observe us, and how we view ourselves. Will we stay healthy and active? Will we be prepared for later life, both from a financial and safety/security point of view? At the macroscopic level, the growing number of elderly and retired citizens is beginning to severely affect the Social Security system, politics, and other aspects of our daily lives. As the baby boom cohort rapidly enters this age group, the implications for American society will be tremendous.

Trends may also reflect other trends. This is the case with the fear-of-victimization trend. Federal crime data continue to show a downward trend in the number of serious crimes committed in America. However, the rise in random, violent attacks has caused more people to be fearful that they, their families, and their property will be victimized. This fear has led to a new trend in the area of home safety and security. Individuals are now spending millions of dollars each year on items to protect themselves and their homes from accidental and criminal intrusion.

On a more global level, the trend toward instantaneous worldwide communications is changing the way we work and play. During the past century, the telegraph has been replaced by the telephone. In turn, the telephone evolved to the fax machine. Today, the Internet and e-mail are replacing even the telephone for immediate communication and access to information. Given the speed at which the telecommunications industry is evolving, one can only dream about how we will communicate globally in the next decade.

Although each of the above trends is different, they do have commonalities. First, each is a reflection of what is happening in society. Each trend is an outcome of both individual and group attitudes and behaviors. Second, each of the trends is a complex set of perceptions and actions. Trends are the broad parameters in which diverse thoughts and activities occur. Third, there is interconnectivity between trends. Trends are dependent on each other, and a change in one trend will usually effect changes in other trends.

Trends are an essential part of a culture. They show the observer what is going on in a given culture and how individuals think about that culture. Trends not only reflect life, they are part and parcel of it. Above all, they are fun for the applied sociologist to identify and track.

What Are Trends?

Most trends start out as a unique idea or activity that is accomplished by an individual or small group of individuals. As the group grows accustomed to the activity, it becomes part of the members' daily lives. Others who come into contact with the activity will decide whether the concept catches their interest, excites them, or motivates them to do something. Over time, this idea or activity spreads, and other individuals buy into it. The trend will then continue to grow as long as both the existing and new audiences are interested in it.

Trends are not simple ideas or behaviors. They are a complex set of attitudes and actions. Trends are affected by time. They are not overnight occurrences. The trends that we follow today began months or even years in the past and continue to change with time. The original idea or activity may no longer exist or may have changed so dramatically that it is hard to remember what it really was or how it got started. Trends come and go over time. They become very popular, die out, and in many cases, resurface later. Time itself will affect the duration and intensity of a trend. Parents who are worried about the "grunge" fashions their kids are wearing need to remember the hippie look they followed in the 1960s. The fashion is quite similar; now, however, it is the uniform of a different generation.

Above all, trends are dynamic processes that change and adapt to their environments. Most trends evolve out of social situations that are interpreted differently by diverse groups and individuals. Thus, different perceptions of the event may lead to different ways of doing things, which then may develop into different trends. When you take these differences and connect them with other factors, such as aging, trends become as diverse as the groups and cultures following them. Add to this differences in ethnic, religious, educational, political, and economic factors, and the trends will take on different meanings and directions.

▓ Types of Trends

Because trends are dynamic, they can be observed at a number of different levels. When trends affect entire groups, cultures, or societies, they are called macroscopic trends. Macroscopic trends are structural in nature because they influence almost every activity within the group. Aging is an excellent example of a macroscopic trend. Not only does aging influence individual attitudes and actions, it affects the social institutions in a society. An aging society will influence the way people think or act. For example, as the U.S. society ages, there is a growing concern that Social Security will not be able to meet the needs of a growing number of retired individuals. Thus, individuals are beginning to change their attitudes and approach to later life. These people are looking at additional retirement/savings plans or thinking about delaying their retirement. Many are living in fear that their old age needs will not be met. These responses affect people's lifestyles and attitudes. Therefore, the aging trend directly or indirectly affects all aspects of the individual's life.

Another macroscopic trend is economics. Almost every activity performed in a society is related to this trend. Economic recession, as evidenced in the 1980s, influenced both behavior and attitudes. Not only did people buy less, they felt less and less secure about their current and future economic well-being. In the 1990s, the overall economy improved and brought with it changes. But as with most macroscopic trends, certain components of the trend advanced faster than others. For example, economic indicators have demonstrated the end of the recession and stable economic growth. However, many people in this country still feel that their personal economic situation is recessionary, and that they and their families are not much better off than they were years ago. This is known as cultural or trend lag. The behavioral component of the trend has progressed faster than the attitudinal component. This causes individuals to wonder if they are part of the dominant trend or an exception to it.

Most of the trends that we share on a daily basis are on the mesoscopic (middle) or microscopic level. These trends affect smaller segments of the population known as interest groups. These groups tend to have unique interests, activities, and lifestyles. For example, the trend toward high-technology home entertainment appeals to certain consumer segments such as the young and highly educated. Internet use, although becoming more mainstream, is still dominated by "hackers," who view it as a form of recreation or a hobby.

To confuse matters, most trends cannot be simply identified as a macro-, meso-, or microlevel trend. As trends move through their lifesyle trajectory, they will also move between the various levels. Many trends start out on the micro level and evolve into meso- or macrolevel trends. Conversely, a trend may become overly specialized or lose its attraction and have only a small group following it. In this case, the trend may revert back to the micro level.

Even with the constant changes, trend levels are convenient ways to identify and locate trends within a group or a culture. They allow the sociologist to place the trends in a hierarchy and then understand the interactivity between a number of trends across and within each of the levels.

※ Trend Life Cycle

Trends do not exist in a vacuum. Trends influence other trends and, in turn, are influenced by them. When trends share this reciprocal relationship, we talk of trend networks. Trend networks are complex systems in which changes in one component trend will affect each of the other trends and the network as a whole. Understanding trend networks is as important as understanding actual trends. As trends grow and develop, they will connect with other trends. This interconnectivity will then create other new trends. This cascading effect not only creates new trends; it also helps to keep the respective trend contemporary and adaptable to an ever-changing social environment.

Like trends, trend networks are dynamic processes. They grow, change directions, become institutionalized, and in many cases, decline and die out. It is important to understand each of these phases in order to respond accurately to the trend. A number of typologies can be used to define the stages in a trend's life cycle. Most typologies assume that a trend will be conceived, grow, and then become institutionalized or decline. These models also assume that trends will naturally progress to a more complex stage. However, although these types of theories may be useful in describing phenomena, they may not always reflect real life. Trends do not necessarily move in straight trajectories from inception to institutionalization. They may grow in popularity, become dormant, grow again, and then fade out. They may also resurface at a later date in some other shape or form.

One of the simplest models to use consists of a four-stage trend life cycle typology. The first stage, inception, is actually the gestational period and birth of a trend. In this situation, a response to a stimulus causes a new idea or action to emerge. This response meets needs in such a way that the individual finds satisfaction, heightens curiosity, and finds a sense of adventure in doing so. The conditions allow the trend to nurture and develop. The actual speed at which the development will occur is based on how quickly the message spreads.

Thus, the inception stage needs a few key elements to fall into place to help the trend evolve. It needs a response to stimuli (social condition, lifestyle, etc.) that is viewed with favor and interest by the participants. The response must meet needs and be viewed as a satisfactory way to think or act. The participant must want to perform this activity again and must want to spread the trend to others. The credibility of the trend and the people associated with it will cause others to imitate the behavior. As the phenomenon spreads, it gains popularity and mass appeal and takes on trend status.

The second stage of the life cycle is growth. During this stage, the trend spreads and begins to take root. Others follow the trend either through direct interaction with or by emulating role models. Role models are very important in that they help others to develop an awareness of the trend. In doing so, they help to shape and form the trend's definition and trajectory. Thus, the "twist" that the role models place on the trend will define how the trend should be played out and whether it will gain mass appeal.

If enough followers exist, the trend will begin to spread to the overall population. As more individuals follow the trend, others are likely to want to be a part of it. A good example of this is the role that the media and sport celebrities play in American culture. We know all about these individuals, and many people want to think, dress, and act just like them. After all, they are successful, and we would not mind having their status and popularity.

The mass appeal and growth of the trend can lead to the third stage, which is institutionalization. The trend has become so popular that it is accepted as part of the normal day-to-day living in the group or culture. An example of this is the blue jeans phenomenon. Once considered the uniform of a generation, it has become so internalized into American culture that it is not uncommon to see three generations (children, parents, and grandparents) all wearing this cultural icon. The institutional stage is a vital point in the trend's life cycle. It is at this time that the trend reaches its peak, changes directions, or declines. Remember that as the trend ages, it will take on different meanings for different groups. Each group will take what it wants from the trend and adapt that to its unique needs and lifestyles. By doing so, group members give the trend a new, but different, life.

As the trend progresses through the institutional stage, it will eventually reach the revitalization/decline stage. During this stage, attempts may be made to reignite interest in the trend. If the interest is not there, the trend will decline and die. If the interest is rekindled, the trend will continue to exist but most likely in a different shape or form.

It is important to remember that the revitalized trend will not be iden-tical to the original trend. To regain appeal and generate new followers, it will have to be adapted to current tastes and interests. Therefore, it could be argued that the trend is actually a new trend and at the incep-tion stage of the life cycle.

▨ Models of Change

As with all aspects of human social behavior, there are a number of ways that change can be viewed. Each of these theories or models takes a unique view or perspective of the change. One must remember that these models serve to place the change agent, such as a trend, into some kind of analytical framework. Because change is dynamic, no one theory or model will yield a complete explanation of what the change is, why it occurred, and what its outcome will be. Therefore, it is best to use a number of models to get a more thorough and accurate view of the change. This process is called *triangulation*.

Many sociologists follow a theory of social change in which each step in the event or phenomenon progresses or evolves to a more com-plex stage. This model has commonly been called *linear evolutionary the-ory*. It is linear because changes are believed to progress almost in a straight line. It is evolutionary because each step along the way is more complex than the one before it. One easy way to view this model is to think of a series of stacks of blocks laid from left to right. The first stack has only one block, the second one two, the third one three, and so on. Each new stack of blocks is built on the existing foundation of blocks. Thus, each stack is progressively larger and more complicated, but each is built on the strength (history, culture) of the previous one. This theory has traditionally been used to explain large-scale or macroscopic changes that occur in a society over time. Many sociologists have used the linear evolutionary model to explain how societies have progressed from simple hunting and gathering groups to the complex structures we live in today.

For example, suppose we wanted to study the long-term effects of technology from the Industrial Revolution until the end of the 20th cen-tury. Using linear evolutionary theory, we could chart a trajectory that shows that as the technology advanced, so did other advancements in society, such as the standard of living. However, our research would also show that with each major technological change came more complexities in relationships, division of labor, and problems in the society.

A criticism of linear evolutionary theory is that it assumes that change will not deviate from a straight-line progression. This is not totally realistic, especially at the mesoscopic and microscopic levels, where change will tend to ebb and flow regularly and not always in the same direction. Thus, linear theory appears to be at its best when used to explain large-scale changes over a longer period of time. It becomes limiting when you are trying to explain why certain factors appear to regress, or be going backward, in a society.

Another way to look at social change is to use a *cyclical* model. This model is probably best summed up in the saying, "what goes around, comes around." In other words, large-scale societal change tends to follow a circular trajectory over time. A good example of cyclical change today is the trend toward family values. Many groups, especially the religious right, are espousing a movement back toward the values they remember from earlier generations. Individuals following this trajectory feel that a movement in this direction would help to resolve many of the contemporary problems facing society today. Also, associated with the older value structure is a nostalgic view of the past, where life is remembered as being slower and easier to deal with.

One of the problems with cyclical theories of social change is that as society has progressed and changed with time, it is virtually impossible to go back exactly to the past you remember. Time, age, social dynamics, attitudes, and customs have changed over the years so that the past is really nostalgically defined in contemporary terms. Think about how your perceptions of an event in your life have changed as you have gotten older. You may think the event was bigger than what it really was, and you may exaggerate the role you played in it. For these reasons, most cyclical changes cannot be viewed as being circular, that is, the changes never really end up back in the same place that they were. A more contemporary model of cyclical change that is receiving attention today is *chaos theory*. The first time you probably heard of this theory was in the movie *Jurassic Park*. However, the theory has been around for years. If cyclical theory posits that "what goes around, comes around," then chaos theory would extend the logic to say that "what goes around, comes around, but not in the same place."

Using our discussion of family values, one quickly realizes that the values of the past will be adapted to the current social environment. Because the environment has changed over time, so will our perceptions of the values. Thus, although the change has, to some degree, been cyclical, the outcome is different from what it originally was in the past. A good way to think of this theory is to use the spiral binding on one of your notebooks. Although each loop appears to be circular, it really does not complete the circle; instead, it evolves into another loop, and the whole process moves forward.

The rather simplistic discussion of change models above has been presented to show you that there are different ways to view the world. As an applied sociologist, you will want to use each of these theories to observe phenomena and come up with explanations that are accurate and actionable.

※ Research Tools

There are a number of research tools that the sociologist can use to analyze and understand change. These range from studying historical events to undertaking actual surveys of individuals to ascertain their perceptions of change and the effect that it is having on them. Both of these tools can be very powerful and can complement each other. The historical analysis provides the background and foundation for understanding the change, whereas the survey will allow you to develop a clearer picture of how individuals currently perceive and adapt to it.

Historical analysis requires the researcher to place him- or herself at earlier points in time to get a feel for what was going on and how these events/attitudes led to the current state of affairs. To do this, the researcher will need to pore over old articles, reports, journals, and videos to develop a hypothesis of why the change occurred. What trends or events caused people to act or think differently? How did these factors build on themselves over time? What model or perspective did the trajectory of the change tend to follow? Was it linear-evolutionary, cyclical, or even chaotic?

Because articles and reports can take on the political perspective of the individual or group writing them, it is important for the researcher to try to substantiate or verify the information. One good way to do this is through a series of interviews with individuals living prior to and during the period of change. What is their recollection of the events that led up to the change? How did the change come about? What is their evaluation of the consequences or outcome of the changes? Ideally, some of these interviews should be with the change agents, that is, those individuals that were directly involved in shaping and directing the change. At the same time, it is also very important to get the opinions of ordinary people who were affected by the change.

One of the hardest things for most researchers to do is to try to view history from the perspective of the participants and not from their own attitudes and values. Trying to judge whether events and actions were necessary years in the past can be misleading, especially if the researcher is looking at it only from his or her current perspective. Therefore, it is very important that the researcher step outside of his or her normal thinking and attempt to place him- or herself in the situation being studied. One's perspective of the past will be much more meaningful if the researcher can actually take on the role of the participants who lived through the event or change. However, this can be very difficult, because we have been socialized to our current environment, and the collection of values and attitudes we have internalized will, by definition, affect how we try to view the world.

Once a review of the past has been accomplished, it is very beneficial to ascertain how individuals are viewing their current situations. Survey research can be used to identify major trends in society and, more importantly, to ascertain the influence that these trends are having on individuals, their families, and their social environments. It is important here to make sure that you survey a representative sample of individuals influenced by the trend or change. If the trend is macroscopic, affecting most of society, you will want to develop and survey a nationally representative sample of people. Similarly, if the change or trend is smaller and more localized, you will want to make sure that you talk to representatives of all the groups affected. By not talking to a good cross-section of respondents, or by selecting the wrong group, you run the risk of receiving erroneous or even biased information.

Probably the best method available today to interview a good cross-section of individuals is the telephone survey. The technology used in telephone surveys allows you to identify regions and populations to whom you want to talk and then dials random telephone numbers of individuals meeting your criteria. A well-written questionnaire will provide you with a great deal of information in a short amount of time. And, although many people are bothered by unsolicited phone calls, most are willing to state their opinion if they feel that the research is valid.

▧ Presentation Tools

Making presentations on trends and social change can be very exciting and creative. Because the subject matter is dynamic, the presentation should be as well. Today's technology offers the presenter a number of tools that will allow the audience to interact directly with the presentation. Unlike many of the other presentations, a presentation on trends and change can use a number of multimedia techniques. For example, if you want to show changes in fashion trends from the 1960s to today, you could show how fashions have changed by using a series of pictures from popular magazines from 1960 to the present. If you wanted to make the presentation a little more dramatic, you could find old television clips where the commentator is talking about the current fashion trend and the impact it was having on society (be it positive or negative). Going one step further, you could take movie clips during the time period and show how the fashions have changed.

Music is another useful tool to use in demonstrating trends and change. Select popular music from each of the time periods under investigation and show how the music has changed with time. Have the audience relate the first thing that comes to mind when they hear a particular song. What were they doing at the time? What were the key social and personal issues they were facing? What styles of clothes were they wearing? How long was their hair? Have them do this across a number of songs from different time periods and look for commonalities. Now, see whether this information supports the other trend information that you have. By doing this, you have included the audience in the presentation and made the presentation more meaningful.

Finally, if you have the ability and the resources, trend presentations are well suited for a variety of multimedia presentations. Changes in society or trends are usually easier to comprehend if the audience can see tangible evidence of the change. This allows them to internalize the change and define it in their own terms. Because many of the people in the audience have lived through and are living through the trends and changes, their interest will be piqued if they feel they are a part of the research and the presentation.

▧ Sociologist as Expert

Identifying trends and interpreting change are roles that sociologists should find interesting and challenging. Training in social theory and research methodology provides the sociologist with the perspective, discipline, and tools to successfully interpret social phenomena and their impact on individuals and groups in a society. Understanding the social environment gives the sociologist the advantage of placing the trend in a social context. This social context helps to better define the trend and explain the impact of other social factors on the trend.

The media and business world have been inundated with so-called change experts and trend gurus. Few, if any, of these experts have the training or backgrounds that sociology majors do. If anything, they have used sociological concepts (whether they knew it or not) to gain their status. They have defined themselves as experts in the areas of change and trend analysis and have been able to sell this impression to others. Because others now believe these individuals to be experts, they go to them for opinions and explanations. By doing so, they give credence to the notion that these people are the experts. In a sense, trend experts have socially constructed reality, and whether or not they have the knowledge or expertise, they now become defined by society as the experts.

Predicting change and defining trends can be very rewarding endeavors. Some of the best known trend gurus make millions of dollars each year through writing books and consulting for businesses and industries. In many cases, the trends defined are at such a macroscopic level that even if the experts' assessment of the trend is not totally correct, they can point to some aspect that they got correct and reinforce their role as experts. Because they continue to sell the fact that they got things right, they are constantly hired to predict the future.

All of these factors lead to the fact that sociologists are the best suited to be the experts in trend analysis and change. However, we must learn how to sell ourselves and our expertise. Traditionally, this has been an area that sociologists have been leery of entering for fear of losing objectivity or biasing their work. The risk here, however, is that others are defining change and trends incorrectly, and these explanations become real in their consequences.

※ Case Study

The Problem

A local newspaper is interested in doing a series of articles on the effects of aging on the population in their community. The newspaper wants to understand how this trend is currently affecting the community and what the likely impact will be over the next 20 to 25 years.

Because of your background in applied sociology, the newspaper has hired you as its resident consultant/expert. Management wants you to provide them with background data on the aging trend in the community. More importantly, they want you to survey the community to obtain the opinions about the trend from both community leaders and local citizens.

Possible Solutions

Background

1. Go to the regional census data repository for the area under investigation. This facility is usually affiliated with one of the universities in or around the community.
   a. Obtain census tract data on the community and map out those areas, if any, where older citizens currently reside. (current)
   b. Next, map out those areas where middle-aged and younger adults reside. (future)
   c. Use your maps and the census data to show the median age of the population today and where it is projected to be 20 years from now.
2. Check with any local agencies that deal with the issues of aging. Obtain any information and projections that they may have.
3. Check to see whether there are any individuals who serve as aging advocates in the community, and interview them to get their perspective on the trend, in general, and the effects on the community, in particular.
4. Take all of the information you have gathered from the above sources and develop an aging profile of the community. This will be beneficial in a number of ways. First, it will serve as good background information for the reporters to develop their stories and gain additional leads for information. Second, this information will allow you to segment the community into key groups that you will want to investigate in more detail.

Community Assessment

Identify key businesses or services in the community that will be affected by an aged population. Locate key people in these groups, and ascertain their views about the future and how they are currently preparing for it. At minimum, you will want to talk with:

1. City government—How will they handle increased services to the elderly with a diminishing tax base? How will they handle aging housing stock?

2. Police—What plans do they have in place to protect a group that will be very concerned about its personal security?

3. Social agencies—How will they handle the increased demand for their services?

4. Businesses—How will the local businesses handle an aging workforce? How will the businesses handle the severe impact on their retirement and pension funds?

Social Survey

1. Based on the accumulated information, develop a survey research strategy that will allow you to interview a broad cross-section of citizens in the community.

2. The first step should be a communitywide survey that will encompass a good demographic cross-section of residents in the community. Make sure that individuals from a variety of age, race, gender, and income groups (social stratification) are interviewed.

   a. Probably the simplest and most efficient research tool to use is a telephone survey.

   b. The survey should focus on respondents' overall views on aging, the perspective on their own aging situation, how they feel the community is dealing with aging, and what they think will have to be done to deal with the aging population in the future.

3. Gather, tabulate, and analyze the results of the survey. Add this information to your ongoing community profile as an additional piece that supports or refutes the other data and opinions received.

4. Finally, if there are some additional questions, or if more in-depth information is needed, create a series of focus groups to enrich the quantitative data. Make sure that these groups are made up of individuals from at least three different age cohorts. First, mature citizens are needed to give their perspective on the current situation. Next, middle-aged residents are needed to discuss their views about what the situation will be like when they become seniors. Finally, a group of young adults is needed to probe for their feelings on the social and economic costs that they will have to bear in order to maintain services for the aged in the future.

Using the Data

A word of caution is needed here. Because you are working for a newspaper, it is natural that the reporters will want to talk with some of the people you interviewed. It is your responsibility to protect the respondents' confidentiality and to maintain the integrity of the research.

1. Make sure that you work out all the study criteria with the client before you enter into the actual research.
2. Maintain the confidentiality of your data sources. Do not give names or telephone numbers without the express permission of the respondent.
3. Tell your respondents that the client may want to contact them directly for additional information. Remind them that doing so is their choice. In the case of the newspaper, you may want to identify (with permission) who the client is so that the respondents will be able to decide whether they want their opinions made public. If any respondent does not wish to participate in these additional interviews, remove his or her name from the list and ask the client to not pursue the respondent any further.

▨ Exercises

1. Interview your parents or grandparents. Ask them about the major changes that have occurred during their lifetimes. Find out how these changes have directly affected their personal lives and how they view the consequences of these changes. Do they see the changes as good, bad, or indifferent? Why?

Next, pick one area of change and probe a little deeper. Was the change macroscopic or microscopic? Did the change occur over a short period of time, or did it take place over a number of years? Did the change immediately affect their lives, or was the influence felt over a longer period of time? How did the individual or family react to the change? What were the benefits or consequences of the change? Looking back, in retrospect, would the individual deal with the change differently today than in the past?

2. Look at the current trends in popular music. How do the trends differ by age and other demographic variables? What effect, if any, does the music have on current attitudes and behaviors? How is this music trend related to other trends in society?

Next, take your favorite form of popular music and trace its growth over time. Where did this style of music come from (i.e., ethnic backgrounds, social class, age groups)? Which groups identify themselves with the music? Are there any historical or social events that are usually associated with the music? What lifestyle or life cycle trends are reflected in the music? Has the style of music changed since its inception? How do you see the music changing in the future?

3. Imagine yourself 50 years in the future. Develop a scenario of what you think life will be like then. What trends that exist today do you think will affect this view of the future? How will they affect it? What will you be doing 50 years from now? How do you envision getting there?

Deviating From the Norm: Good News and Bad News

Deviance, like beauty, is in the eye of the beholder. Although this statement may sound somewhat strange, it is actually very true. Like beauty, deviance is socially and culturally defined. It is a response to a norm, that is, a socially accepted pattern of behavior. However, because social behavior is not set in concrete, individuals and groups will interpret norms in any number of ways. Thus, what is considered socially acceptable by one group may as easily be viewed as deviant behavior by others. For example, look at the relatively brief 50-year history of rock-and-roll music. When rock-and-roll music gained public attention in the early 1950s, it was met with outcries from numerous groups in society that viewed the music as anti-Christian and antipatriotic. In their minds, this music was going to destroy family values and the American way of life. Not only did rock and roll question the socially accepted norms for music, dance, and public propriety, it also called into question long-held attitudes and norms on racism and sexual activity.

One would have thought that the years following the beginning of rock and roll would have turned this "deviant" behavior into socially accepted behavior. However, each subsequent generation of rockers since the 1950s has had to deal with the label of deviant. The irony of this is that the group once considered to be the deviants became the normative group that labeled the next group as deviants. The Elvis Presley generation looked askew at the "Beatles" generation, who in turn had problems with "acid rock," "alternative rock," and so on. Thus, each step in the evolution of this musical form was beset by a label of deviance, with this deviance usually being defined by a group of people who were themselves labeled deviant by their predecessors.

It is important to remember that behavior that deviates from the norm can be dysfunctional to the group but can also be an agent for change. Breaking rules may be a sign that some individuals and groups do not share the same normative definitions, or they have decided to replace the socially approved means to an end with their own perspectives and behaviors. Thus, bank robbers may accept the societal definition of having a lot of money. However, the socially approved norms of hard work, saving, and investment may be replaced with the quick fix of obtaining this wealth through unacceptable means.

On the other hand, if large groups in society do not adhere to the norm, it may signal that changes in attitudes and behaviors have occurred and that the existing norms may need to be redefined or changed altogether. For example, in the 1960s, many states passed laws stating that individuals could not wear clothes made from an American flag or replicas of it. This was done in response to the various student, racial, and women's groups that were questioning the existing social order in the United States. The group in power felt that wearing the flag was defacing it and what it stood for and thus passed laws (socially accepted norms) to eliminate this unpatriotic behavior. Today, however, it is quite common to see many groups, ranging from the conservative religious groups to athletes to rockers wearing attire that replicates the American flag. In most of these cases, this is done as a sign of identification and patriotism. It is possible that many of the original laws have not been changed, so that people wearing American flag regalia today out of identification and patriotism may, in reality, be committing a deviant and criminal act. The irony of this is that the deviant behavior today actually supports the intent of the original law.

As applied sociologists, we are less concerned with the "badness" of the deviance. We are more concerned with the conditions and the definitions that cause the deviance to exist. We also want to know how various individuals and groups respond to the non-normative behavior. Most importantly, we want to be able to understand the impact of the behavior on the group, culture, and society.

▧ What Is Normative Behavior?

As we have mentioned in earlier chapters, social behavior is, for the most part, structured, patterned, and expected. It is structured in order to place some boundaries or parameters around individual behavior. This process is known as social control. The intent is to develop some order to the group or society. For example, all of us are familiar with a red, octagonal sign that we see at intersections. Even if it did not have any writing on it, we know that this means that we are to bring our vehicle to a stop before continuing through the intersection. The intent of this sign (and, therefore, the norm) is to maintain social order. What would happen if there were no stop signs? The number of accidents, injuries, and even deaths would go up dramatically. Think how much your car insurance would cost!

Social behavior is patterned. Certain jobs or positions in society function because there are behaviors associated with them. These social roles and statuses are dependent upon the player and the rest of the participants sharing the same definitions of the behaviors. These socially agreed-upon attitudes and behaviors become ways of thinking or acting as defined by the group. Norms can run the gamut from the way one dresses (folkways) to the way groups morally view the behavior (e.g., Ten Commandments) to behavior with legal sanctions and punishment. As with most social behavior, norms are complex and cross a number of levels. Wearing a bikini swimsuit to your wedding would probably be considered to be in bad taste (folkway), but there are probably no laws that prohibit you from doing so. Now, let us say that you do wear the swimsuit into the church. The minister and other individuals come up to you and tell you that your behavior is immoral and that you are committing a mortal sin. You have now broken both a folkway and the mores (moral sanctions). Finally, the police are called and you are arrested for indecent exposure and creating a public disturbance. Now, you have broken the law!

Finally, socially conforming behavior is expected. Because the norms are the shared definitions of behaviors, we come to expect individuals and groups to play out those behaviors in mutually shared ways. Not only does this maintain order, it allows us to develop a comfort zone in which we are able to expect and anticipate the behavior that is to occur. By expecting the normative behavior, we are able to develop responses to it in an orderly, shared manner. Think of a classroom and the expected behavior for the role of teacher and student. When you walk into the classroom, there are certain normative expectations that you have about the teacher even before you have met the individual. You expect the person in the teacher role to impart information, maintain order in the classroom, and evaluate your performance fairly. After many years of attending school, you are so adept at this process that you can assess the teacher in a matter of a few minutes and develop your expectations for the course. By the way the teacher is dressed, presents to the class (reading material verbatim vs. discussing material), and handles questions, you can define pretty quickly your expectations of what the class will be like.

On the other hand, the normative behavior of the classroom has expectations of how you will play out your role as student. Most classrooms have the chairs and tables organized neatly. Once you enter the room, you are expected to sit in one of these chairs, and in many cases, you may even be assigned to it. Once a bell rings or the teacher begins to talk, you are expected to be quiet and attentive to the lecture. If you have a question or comment, you are expected to raise your hand and wait patiently to be recognized. Otherwise, you are expected to listen to what the teacher is saying and take notes as appropriate.

⊠ Defining Deviance

At its most basic definition, deviance is the act of not following the norms of the group or society. This sounds pretty simple, but as a sociologist, you have come to expect that most social behavior is not that simple. So, let us look at the concept of deviance in a little more detail. Like socially approved behavior, deviant behavior has to be defined as such by the group or society. This can run the gamut from the statement "We don't do things that way" to codified laws that define what deviance is and how we can expect to be punished for it. Obviously, the level of sanctioning and punishment will be related to the severity that the group places on the deviant act. The deviant act of whispering in class may be sanctioned by only a word or glance from the teacher, whereas the deviant act of murder may be punished by the execution of the offender.

It is important to remember that definitions of deviance are not always understood, shared, or followed by all of the members of a group or society. In many cases, the definitions will differ from group to group, community to community, and state to state. For example, look at the legal ages for driving, smoking, and drinking. Although they may differ from state to state, most states have enacted laws that dictate the socially appropriate age at which one is allowed to legally drive a car, smoke a cigarette, or drink alcohol. This is not to say that individuals are physically incapable of performing these acts before they reach that age. It does say, however, that one can be punished for breaking these norms by being under the socially approved age. This is done to maintain social order and control, and although research is used at times to decide the most appropriate age, one age is often selected arbitrarily over another. A 21-year-old taking an alcoholic drink will not differ that much from a 20-year-old having the same type of alcoholic drink. However, the norms dictate that the 21-year-old can legally drink the alcohol, whereas the 20-year-old is performing deviant behavior.

In many cases, the behavior may not be considered deviant by the group. In the 1960s, many college students felt that smoking marijuana was socially acceptable behavior, even though it was considered a felony in most states and punishable in some cases with up to 50 years in prison. Today, we read and hear a great deal about the use and existence of state militias. Although they share the overall normative aspects of the U.S. Constitution and patriotism, these groups have actually decided that many of the existing laws are contrary to their definition and interpretation of the "American way of life." Therefore, they feel that they have the right to disregard the socially accepted norms and replace them with their own interpretation. This difference of "opinion" becomes very serious when the deviance moves from a singular act of disregarding the norm to any act where the norm is intentionally broken. In this case, the act of civil disobedience may actually cause large-scale damage, injury, and death to other people.

Another key factor in defining deviance is when the group is faced with conflicting norms. Which ones should they follow? Historically, the country of Ireland has been governed by both secular and religious laws. In most cases, these laws were one and the same, so most people had little problem adhering to both sets of laws. However, deep societal changes have been taking place in Ireland over the past 10 years that have resulted in a conflict between religious beliefs and civil laws. A current debate centers on the issue of shops opening for business on Sundays. For the most part, shops close at 5:30 p.m. or 6:00 p.m. most days, and they might stay open until 8:00 p.m. one night of the week. Historically, no shops, with the exception of a limited opening time for newspapers and gasoline businesses, were open on Sunday. This is in conformance with the edicts of the Catholic Church laws. However, a number of internationally owned businesses have established retail outlets in Ireland, and, using the argument that it would make life more convenient for working individuals, a retail/grocery chain announced plans to open on Sundays and to pay the workers triple time pay rates. This was unheard of. The company offered triple time to encourage the workers to come to work. However, looking back on the strategies used by this company, the services of a sociologist might have been useful in explaining social behavior. The Irish Roman Catholic Church (the predominant religious body in the Republic of Ireland) came out fighting to protect the sanctity of the Sunday day of rest. Although staying open on Sunday was not a violation of Irish civil law, it was a definite violation of the religious law. This was a deviant act. The announcement was followed by a national rebuke and warnings about the spiritual dangers of going to the shops on Sunday by the highest Irish official Catholic representative. Local Sunday church services were marked by sermons that preached the need to abide by church laws and the punishments that would follow if the religious norms were violated. The intent to open stores on Sundays started in 1996 and is still under debate in Ireland. A few stores have opened and are quietly doing business.

This is a case in which individuals and groups have to decide which group's norms they will keep. They may agree with the secular norm and actually find it more convenient to go to the stores on Sunday, but they may be fearful of the punishment they will receive from the church for doing so. Although this discrepancy may not sound too traumatic to most Americans, who are used to doing both on Sundays, it is a serious concern to many Irish citizens, who want to be able to shop on Sundays but do not want to deviate from the norms of the church.

Whether or not you think about it, we are constantly in a number of situations similar to the one described above. Our behavior may be defined by a number of norms, and these norms may be in conflict with each other. This may run the gamut, from telling a white lie to get yourself or a friend out of a troubling situation, to deciding the most appropriate behavior in situations (such as having an abortion) that have major legal, moral, and religious implications at the micro, meso, and macro levels of social order.

As applied sociologists, we need to take all of these factors into consideration when we are analyzing deviant behavior. How and why is the behavior being defined as deviant? Who is defining it as deviant? Is the group or individual performing the behavior accepting it as deviant? And, if a number of norms are in conflict with each other, why was one norm chosen over the others? Once again, you will want to place the deviant behavior in a social context and assess the environmental factors affecting it.

The Consequences of Deviance: Bad News/Good News

Deviant behavior can be considered bad news or good news for a group or society. In most cases, we tend to view the deviance as being negative and, in many cases, harmful. But as sociologists, we also need to be aware of the positive effects of some deviant acts. A classic example of this comes from Durkheim's study of suicide. Although he talks about egoistic suicide as being centered on the individual's inability to cope with his or her social environment (negative), he also talks about altruistic suicide, where the individual dies in order to protect the safety and lives of others in the group or society (positive). Even his description of anomic suicide could be viewed as positive, in that a suicidal response to a normless situation will, in and of itself, create norms for dealing with the situation in the future. All three of these types of behavior are deviant behavior. However, as a society, we have defined some types as being more positive or socially acceptable than others.

Probably one of the major negative connotations of deviant behavior is its subsequent disruption of the social order. When groups of individuals are used to doing things in certain ways, deviating from these norms can be disconcerting, confusing, and painful. Not only are the normal, day-to-day activities disrupted, but the group has to change its behavior to respond to the deviant act. We have very strong norms about breaking into a home and stealing another's possessions. These norms are meant to maintain the social order and to provide a sense of security. Thus, the residents can maintain a level of comfort that, under normal circumstances, their house is safe and secure. Although they are aware that something could happen, they are not overly concerned and go about their normal daily activities.

Now, let us say that the house is burglarized. Normal behavior and activity is disrupted. Not only are prized possessions missing, but the victims now feel a loss of the sense of security and a sense of being violated. No longer will they be able to feel totally secure, and they may change their behavior dramatically to ensure their safety in the future. This may mean being more careful, putting in a security system, or even purchasing a weapon. At the same time, the victims will have to change their normal activities in order to focus on solving the crime. They will have to interact with one or a number of police officers, create an inventory of the articles stolen, and deal with their insurance company. Also, they may be asked to go to the police station to identify recovered property, and they may have to appear in court as part of the case against the alleged offender. Thus, the one deviant act may disrupt normative activities both in the present, as they respond to the act, and in the future, as they change lifestyles to protect themselves from the act ever happening again.

Related to the disruption is the fear of victimization. Recent governmental findings have shown that the actual amount of violent crime has declined over the past couple of years. Whether society is becoming less deviant or less deviance is being reported is a subject for another debate. However, it does not appear that individuals have equated the lower incidence of crime with their fear of being victimized. If anything, the feelings that we or someone we know will eventually be victimized have increased dramatically over the years. Thus, even the threat of deviance has caused a change in behavior. Individuals fearful of being victimized will change their normal activities to minimize their chances of being the recipient of a deviant act. This may mean buying devices (i.e., home and car security systems) to warn them of impending deviant acts, or physically changing behavior, such as not going out alone after dark. In either case, just the threat of deviance has changed behavior and lifestyles and disrupted the existing normative behavior.

A third consequence of the deviant behavior is the labeling process that usually accompanies it. Once a deviant act occurs and an individual or group is associated with it, it is quite common for members of society to label the alleged offenders as deviant, whether they are guilty or not. For example, look at the O. J. Simpson case. Whether you personally agree or disagree about his innocence, it is safe to say that most of American society has labeled him guilty of murder. Once the label is attached, the way that person acts and how others act with him or her change dramatically. Because most people have labeled Simpson as a murderer, even though the legal system found him innocent, his lifestyle and livelihood have changed dramatically. Not only has he lost any acting, commentating, or endorsement opportunities, but he has also been refused entrance into public areas, such as restaurants and golf clubs.

Once the deviant label is attached, it is pretty hard to remove it. Let us say that in the next couple of years, we find out that others were responsible for the murder that Simpson was accused of and that he was actually innocent of the crime. How likely will it be for people in American society to remove the deviant label and accept him the way they did before the crime? Also, how likely will it be that his children will be able to shed the label that they are the son and daughter of a murderer? Because of the immense amount of media coverage of this trial, it is highly unlikely that things can ever return to normal for those involved in the Simpson case.

Finally, one of the positive consequences of deviance is that it may actually be a precursor for change. The act of deviance may be a response to norms that are out of date or practices that are no longer followed or are not socially accepted. Remember, this does not mean that the actual deviant act is acceptable, for it is still violating an existing social norm. After all, Robin Hood was still a thief when he robbed the rich to give to the poor, no matter how commendable this act may have been. The deviant behavior may suggest that there are problems or inequities in the existing system that need to be changed. Keep in mind that the changes brought about by the deviant act may not be viewed as normative behavior by all individuals or groups, and the change in and of itself may cause additional deviance to occur.

◪ Research Tools

There is a wide array of research tools from which to choose. However, your criteria for selecting a research tool should be based on your research design and your study objectives. You will find data for your study in many different places, which would strongly support our recommendation for the use of multiple data collection methods to gather a more accurate and detailed view of your study topic.

In terms of ease, secondary data collection is your first choice. Using this research skill, you will most likely gather data from newspaper stories and TV news and video archives. However, a tremendous source of unreported news can be found on many different national and international addresses on the Internet. New sites are appearing daily, and government agencies are beginning to make some data available through the Internet. Examples of deviance do not sit on the park bench waiting to be discovered, and you will most likely gather more data than you need for your analysis. As you include secondary data sources in your analysis, we strongly urge you to check and recheck the accuracy of the data you have gathered. For this reason, collecting data from a number of different publications, verifying the accuracy of the story lines between the publications, and looking for changes in the report over time is our recommended data collection strategy when using secondary data collection techniques. You are probably not the first person to study this topic, and the university/college libraries and local libraries carry a wide variety of information on your topic of interest. The beauty of Internet technology is the ability to track down and order the work of authors and publications of interest in a fraction of the time it would have taken 5 years ago.

If you are thinking of conducting a detailed study in the area of deviance, you will need to consider some kind of research tool using *observation*. Field studies (i.e., data gathered as the social behavior is taking place, with the investigator present in some capacity at the event) may be the most suitable research strategy to follow. However, *participant observation* is an advanced data collection tool and should be learned under the supervision of a sociologist experienced in this methodology. Briefly, there are four possible ways of gathering data using this strategy.

First, you might select two groups for your study focus. One group would be more likely than the other to display the activities that you have identified in your research design. You do not play any role in these activities. You inform the groups that you are studying their behavior, and you observe and take notes. Second, you decide to become a member of each group and participate in the activity. You inform each group that you are an investigator and that you are participating in their activities. You might find that it is harder to keep track of recording the data using this technique, but you will gain other valuable information from participating. Third, you select two groups for your study. You do not tell them what you are doing, and you observe and take notes. Fourth, you select two groups for study. You become a member of each group. You do not inform anyone of your reason for being in the group. You gather data from your experiences in each of the groups.

We generally refer to the activities of the first two groups as being conducted in an overt manner. The latter two data collection skills use a covert data collection technique. The covert approach is most likely used when the investigator has a deep interest in identifying the social structure, social process, and norms of a secret group or society. However, there are a number of legal issues, such as violating personal rights, entrapment, and personal privacy and business privacy laws. There are plenty of examples of the misuse of covert data collection techniques such as when ambitious television producers or investigative reporters took concealed cameras into areas closed to the public to expose seemingly illegal, or at the very least embarrassing, activities. Many of these stories have resulted in million-dollar lawsuits, which have been settled out of court following the payment of damages. Please remember that your pursuit of accurate data does not include the right to break laws or abuse people's rights. So how do you do a study like this? Look for someone who is a gatekeeper or may have access to the information you are looking for. Approach this individual, explain your research design, and ask for assistance. Finally, this data collection technique requires experience and skill. You may want to find someone who has experience and ask for an opportunity to work with him or her in order to study how the technique is done.

When you cannot get access to the arena of the group you are interested in studying, you can use other methods to gather data. Do not forget the data that can be gathered by carefully examining pictures and video coverage of social behavior. As a result of the increase and development of global communications technology, our ability to gather data and be participant observers of events as they unfold in many areas of the world is greatly enhanced by the advent of 24-hour global cable news coverage and increased use of the Internet. It should be noted that there is an inherent bias in the types of pictures and video feed that are presented on news programs. The pictures are selected on the basis of their impact and may give a misleading representation of the phenomenon being studied. However, from a sociologist's perspective, the presentation of a group's activities in video and broadcast news may be a valuable source of data when discussing the label that is associated with the group. Remember, though, that much of what is squeezed into a brief news broadcast is an overview of the issue and should be regarded as a starting point and not the complete picture. If possible, find video feed and pictures beyond those presented in the evening news that give an overall picture of the phenomenon you are studying.

Personal interviews are considered excellent sources for studying details surrounding the factors that contribute to why people commit deviant behaviors. Interviews can be conducted with personnel such as group leaders, group members, victims, and members of the general public who might be in a position to provide information. Prepare an agenda of questions based on the information you have gathered from your data searches, newspaper reports, television broadcasts, and other sources. You may find that once you start interviewing a person, the information flows in such a way that you do not need to ask specific questions. In any case, make sure that you tape (with permission) each interview and/or take very thorough notes.

Finally, keep in mind throughout your study that you should expect to encounter problems with finding data—any data. The data that you find will have errors and, particularly in the case of news media data, may have been edited and filtered by others. However, if the analysis of social behavior was an easy task, there would be no need for sociologists.

⚅ Presentation Tools

We have discussed the problems associated with data collection. This is a very important issue to keep in mind when preparing your analysis for presentation. Do not let the need to present a brief presentation curtail your data collection efforts. Gather as much data about your topic of interest as you can find. Search for those elusive pieces of data, and make note in your presentation of the difficulties encountered in finding data. As you will no doubt discover, you will have gathered an overwhelming amount of data on which to base your analysis.

Because you do not want people to fall asleep during your presentation, you need to carefully design a presentation that deals with your prioritized points of interest in an interesting and thought-provoking manner. First of all, you need to consider the preparation of a series of different reports designed for different audiences. You may find that your audiences may run the gamut from the general public to an official presentation to a government agency. If at all possible, prepare a multimedia presentation that can be used routinely with boilerplate text adapted for your target audience. The use of illustrative materials that assist you in the identification of normal or deviant behavior, such as photographs, video clips, and any recordings of interview events, are powerful motivators for the audience to focus on your presentation.

Remember that you are planning to present data and findings on the topic of deviance. Your audience may have preconceived opinions and views about this topic before you make your presentation. You may have certain opinions about this topic. However, your responsibility as a sociologist is to present the findings in an objective manner, leaving your personal values out of the presentation. The moral responsibility you have to present your findings in an objective manner is particularly important in situations where the data do not support the general views and opinions of the audience. If you find yourself in the situation of presenting a report that is diametrically opposite the general opinions and views held by your audience, you might want to think about discussing the findings with a smaller audience of principles and prepare them for these findings.

As a sociologist, it is not your job to assign blame but to analyze social behavior. Although not assigning blame, you should feel comfortable pointing out in your report the conditions that are conducive for the emergence of deviant behavior and how social structures and processes can be changed or redesigned to accommodate the emerging deviant behavior or to discourage further deviant acts. Make a brief, concise presentation that focuses on providing answers to the main issues of interest to your audience. Prepare additional information in a multimedia format that will enable you to answer additional questions on areas that might be of interest to the audience. Listen carefully to the questions you are asked, and frame your answers based on the data gathered or on your experience as a sociologist. Avoid the trap of being drawn into a discussion based on value statements and anecdotal examples of deviant behavior.

▧ Sociologist as Expert

As we have discussed in this chapter, deviance is much more than breaking a socially accepted rule or norm. As sociologists, we want to know why this deviance is occurring, how people are responding to it, and what its impact is on individuals, groups, and societies. To do this, one needs to be able to look at a diverse array of factors and ascertain their relationship to the deviant act. The training you have received in sociology should enable you to accomplish this successfully.

As a sociologist, you will quickly understand that the existing norms may be viewed from different perspectives with different definitions. You will automatically begin to develop scenarios on the factors that separate deviant definitions from the more socially accepted one. You will turn to your sociological perspective toolkit to triangulate reasons why the deviance is occurring. From a consensus perspective, you will look for indicators of social structure, process, and control. From a conflict perspective, you will identify who makes and controls the socially accepted definitions and how they are enforced. From an interactionist perspective, you will ascertain how the norms are defined among and across a number of groups.

Also, as a sociologist, you will have the ability to place the deviant behavior in its social context. Is the deviant behavior situationally defined? Is it a response to an unachievable norm, or is it really an acceptable norm within a smaller subculture or group? Because of your skills in looking at the broad picture, you will be able to ascertain the scope and magnitude of the deviance. Is it at the micro level, affecting only the individual committing it, or at the meso level, affecting families, places of work, and communities? Finally, is the deviance of such magnitude that it is influencing society and, potentially, social change?

Probably the greatest advantage that you have as a sociologist in studying deviant behavior is your ability to view the deviant definitions and acts objectively. While we all have our own personal beliefs and feelings, you have been trained to minimize these as you investigate the behavior. This is not to say that you approve of or condone the behavior; it does say that you will take on the role of others while attempting to understand the conditions and motivations that caused the action. Having this skill is extremely important in finding complete and accurate information and then applying this intelligence to resolve the problem or to help direct public policy making.

⚅ Case Study

The Case

Recent news reports have focused on an arrest in a rural county in the heartland of America. Five individuals were arrested following a routine evening police stop for speeding. A subsequent search of the vehicle yielded a sophisticated cache of weapons: large automatic weapons, assault rifles, pistols, hand revolvers, manufactured and handmade ammunition, night vision goggles, gas masks, and a fully operational sophisticated wireless communications system. The five arrested, three men and two women, were wearing full camouflage uniforms. Papers gathered in the search of the vehicle detailed plans for exploding a series of pipe bombs at the local power station. The five individuals were released on bail pending their trial. No one showed up on the day of the trial. Instead, a press release by the public relations director of a militia organization stated that these five individuals were conducting the legal business of their organization and that the court in which they had been asked to appear did not have any legal jurisdiction over them.

Most new members of militia organizations are required to take an oath that includes such promises as a pledge to abide by the rules and constitution of their own states; an agreement to obey all legal laws—federal, state, and local; a promise to protect and defend America from all foreign and domestic enemies; and a vow of allegiance to the Constitution. There appears to be both norm conflict here and the potential for acts of deviance and perhaps criminal acts of destruction.

As a sociologist, you have been asked to make a presentation to a small regional committee of criminal justice professionals. The purpose of your presentation is to educate this group on the need for the inclusion of a social science component in their plan for the establishment of a Tactical Terrorist Response Unit in the region. The establishment of this unit has been mandated by the federal government in response to recent, unexplained incidents, such as the one just described here. You have 2 weeks to prepare your presentation. You are responsible for all costs incurred in the preparation of this report.

Possible Solutions

Deviance is generally defined as the violation of social norms in a society. As you have learned in this chapter, studying deviance is not as easy as it appears. The usual studies of deviance center on acts of criminal justice where the line between legal and illegal is seemingly clear and identifiable. We are going to use a different kind of example here to encourage you to stretch your skills of analysis in an area where there is a wealth of data to access. Remember that you are not preparing a presentation that is designed to inform about militia; rather, you are preparing a presentation that demonstrates the contribution that a social science perspective can bring to the proposed task force unit. Once again, we strongly recommend that you use a multimethod approach.

Identification of the Phenomenon

What has been presented to you in this case study is one of the most complex issues facing American society today. Your audience will most likely have an interpretation of the concept of "militia" that is influenced by their concern for social control issues in society. Your task is to expand this perspective to permit the understanding of how social groups work and increase the skill of differentiating illegal acts of rebellion from legal acts of protest.

Social groups. Develop a brief report that reviews the sociological research about the formation of social groups and organizations and the criteria for the presence of deviance from the social norms of society in certain groups. Your report should include a description of the role of the members of fringe organizations in the maintenance and structure of the central social group.

Social movements. Prepare a brief report that reviews the formation of social movements and the criteria for deviance in these groups.

Cultural issues of interest. Review and prepare a brief report on research into the current intense interest in the approach of the new millennium and the rhetoric of doom and activism.

Terrorism. Define the term *terrorism,* making sure that you deal with the topic of increasing interest—the threat of domestic terrorism.

Militia or patriot. Define the term *militia.* This is not as easy a task as it sounds. You will need to sharpen your knowledge of the wording and interpretation of the Second Amendment to the Constitution regarding the right to bear arms and the important role that this plays in the mission and objectives of the militia movement. You will need to review your history archives to familiarize yourself with the history of the militia movement. What are the differences between the old and new militia movements? You will also need to include a report dealing with the differentiation between the terms *patriot* and *militia.* What are the criteria by which you, as a sociologist, would assess the potential for violence by a militia group?

Sociological research skills. Present a brief overview of the sociological skills that can be used to provide data and continuous analysis (e.g., the use of case study methodology, content analysis, multivariate data techniques, interviewing skills, and analysis of indicators from the sociological perspective).

Justification of the Need for a Sociologist's Perspective in the Task Force Unit

Having presented the previously described sociological concepts, you will be in a position to present a justification that is based on the contributions that a sociologist can make to the proposed program.

- The ability to build a comprehensive sociological database based on regional demographics and access to current data
- The ability to place deviant behavior in its social context and provide assistance with identifying the scope and magnitude of the deviant behavior
- The ability to formulate and coordinate regional analyses of the potential for an increase or decrease in deviant behavior

Tentative Plan and Proposed Budget

Prepare a proposal on how you would go about making a contribution as a sociologist to the new proposed task force and an estimate of the resources that will, at a minimum, be necessary for the project. It is extremely important to inform the committee that much of the data currently available is not always the most accurate, and that analysis based on erroneous data is sometimes worse than no data at all.

▧ Exercises

The study of deviant social behavior is best conducted using a multimethod approach. If at all possible, the best way to gain an understanding of how social groups are organized and what constitutes deviance is to conduct an intense, detailed study of a group. The following exercises are designed to help you begin to understand the various layers of analysis that need to be completed before you can begin to answer questions about deviance. These exercises make use of basic research skills such as case study analysis, secondary data analysis, and content analysis of news and print media. One of the major problems sometimes facing an investigator studying a topic such as this is how to conduct an objective study in an area where the investigator has strong personal opinions. This is a difficult assignment, but mastery of the research skills you are learning will go a long way toward assisting you to gather objective, empirical data.

1. Select four social groups for a small case study. Select two of the groups on the basis of their identity as mainstream American social groups. Select two other groups that are not identified as members of mainstream America. Identify the mission, goals, and objectives of each group. Compare and contrast the norms of each group. Compare and contrast the ritualism of each social group. Rate each group in terms of its capacity for being traditional or innovative, ritualistic or nonritualistic, rebellious or conservative. Finally, on the basis of the analysis you have just conducted, rank each group from normal to deviant.

What else do you think needs to be included in this analysis?

2. Identify three groups whose public image can be attributed to the tenets of labeling theory. Track the development of the label associated with the group. Find and describe the nature of any threats to the label presently enjoyed by any of these social groups. For example, 10 years ago, televangelists enjoyed the label and positive image of doing God's work and millions of dollars in donations. However, a number of televangelists and their organizations became the targets of intense media scrutiny into the personal behavior of the organization officers and the financial affairs of the organization. Many of these televangelist organizations did not survive the investigations.

3. Most of us went through our school experience wanting to be a member of the "in" crowd. Some of us wanted to be members of other kinds of groups. What is the difference between a good gang and the other kind of gang? (This exercise is not as easy as it appears. You will be tempted to answer in an emotional manner. Frame your answer, including personal observations, using your skills as a sociologist.)

4. We have always been told that police officers are sworn to uphold the law. On the other hand, other social control forces, such as the FBI and CIA, may become involved in activities (e.g., wiretapping, searching a suspect's home, and video and surveillance techniques) that do not appear, on the surface, to be upholding the law.

Based on what you have learned about deviant behavior, how would you explain the behavior of the groups we have described here?

Making Sense out of the Unexpected

As sociologists, we are very much aware of the fact that all human be-havior is not totally predictable. Many aspects of social life fall into the category of "unexpected events." As with other sociological phenom-ena, unexpected events can be viewed across the various levels of socio-logical analysis. Let us use an example here to illustrate this point. You get an emergency call from your child's school stating that a couple of the students were found with medical kits they had stolen from a doctor's office. The needles used for injections were missing, and a number of other students had complained about these two students randomly sticking them with the needles. Students are hysterical, and a number of parents are panic-stricken. Both the police and emergency medical staff are on-site at the school. The caller asks you to come to the school, pick up your child, and take him or her to your family doctor immediately.

This crisis or unexpected event has ramifications on a number of levels. On the micro level, you are very concerned about your child's health. With the information that you have heard about the transmittal of diseases such as HIV and hepatitis through blood, you are terrified about what could possibly happen to your child and your family. On the meso level, you are concerned about the effect of this event on the school. What could the school have done to prevent this from happen-ing? How will it deal with this current problem? What will be both the short-term and long-term effects on parents sending their children to this school? On the macroscopic level, if diseases are transmitted in the school, will they spread to the larger community? How will the community react to this unexpected event? Will people treat it as an isolated incident or as behavior of epidemic proportions?

As you can see, this event affects us in a number of ways across a number of levels. Because of the unexpected nature of many of these events, traditional sociologists have, in most cases, shied away from the area of collective behavior that is not regular, patterned, and normative. As applied sociologists, we feel that it is very important for you to be able to identify and place meaning on collective behavior that is unexpected and different from normal, day-to-day behavior. You will find this information useful in helping you understand emergency situations and dealing with crisis management. This might take the form of dealing with a tragic fire to a house or business in your neighborhood; a series of events that call for the emergency resources of many community agencies (e.g., fires, floods, and blizzards); traumatic changes in the business environment (e.g., stock market crashes); or national and international events that you see on television or read about in the newspaper.

▧ Why Study Unexpected Events?

Thankfully, the occurrence of unexpected events such as disasters (either natural or man-made), emergencies, and crises are infrequent, but their existence provides the perfect arena for us to study sociological perspectives and processes at work in dynamic situations. When these unexpected events do occur, we want to be able to explain how and why the social behavior occurred, and, more importantly, the outcome or effect of this behavior. Also, apart from an academic interest in these events, researchers are also anxious to provide information to assist in better planning and preparations to avoid the recurrence of such an event. Fires in your neighborhood, explosions in the chemical factory on the other side of town, the announcement that the main employer in the area is closing down its business, a gunman who takes a school hostage, or a plane that crashes are just a few examples of unexpected events that may directly or indirectly affect you, your family, your community, or your society. During the winter of 1997-1998, we watched states on the West Coast make preparations for the expected outcomes of the highly publicized weather phenomenon called El Niño. Based on lessons learned from prior experiences with this potentially devastating weather system, local state and federally funded and approved programs were put in place to help people prepare for this event and minimize the damage it could cause.

Examples of unexpected events can be found in diverse settings or organizations, or in the response of individuals in society to perceived threats or disruption of their regular social interactions. One of the most powerful recent examples of collective behavior in the United States can be found in the collective response to the events that followed the Alfred P. Murrah Federal Building explosion in Oklahoma City, which claimed 168 lives. The most significant issue surrounding this disaster was that in addition to the impact of the explosion on the lives of those affected by the blast, the sense of security and invincibility that residents of the United States enjoyed until then was destroyed on that day. Although there had been fatal explosions before this, most Americans would not have thought that destruction of this magnitude would happen in an American city. We have seen these things happen in other parts of the world but not in the heartland of America. Also, our perceptions of terrorists changed as we learned that it was Americans, not foreign extremists, who bombed the building. No longer was this event something that happened to others, thousands of miles away, but something that could happen to us and our loved ones.

Thinking of a global example of collective behavior brings immediately to mind the August 1997 car crash in the streets of Paris. That event became the focal point of the most powerful worldwide collective display of grief since the assassination of President John F. Kennedy. Officially, Diana, the Princess of Wales, was an outcast of the British royal family, but worldwide, she was known as "the People's Princess." During the 7 days following her death, we witnessed an unexpectedly overwhelming worldwide public tribute to the late Princess. The public display of emotion during this event has taken its place in history as the singular collective response to a seemingly ordinary car crash. More than 2 billion television watchers joined the estimated 1 million bystanders, along with the 1,600 special invitees gathered in Westminster Abbey, to attend the funeral of a member of English royalty. This came after days of public expressions of mourning in the streets; miles of floral tributes left along the streets of London, in front of the gates of palaces across the country, and in front of British embassies around the world; and the constant coverage of the event on television around the world and at the scene of the accident. It has now been confirmed that the newspaper coverage of the death and funeral of Princess Diana surpassed the former record coverage of the end of World War II. Her death has been described as a "national disaster" and an "international" disaster.

As much as the media are criticized for their intrusion into private lives, the regular transmission of global news, particularly through CNN (and more recently, other networks, such as MSNBC), has moved the activities of the world into our everyday reality. It is interesting to note that CNN, in the United States, carried the news of the death of Princess Diana before the formal announcement was made on the BBC. Turn on CNN at any time of the day or night, in just about any country, and you will become a witness to an unfolding story that may be the precursor to a catastrophic disaster. How many of you remember watching the CNN reporters showing live pictures from their hotel room as Baghdad was being bombed at the beginning of the Gulf War? For the first time in history, you were seeing "real-time" war from behind enemy lines. Also, consider the pictures of the oil wells burning out of control in Kuwait. Not only were you seeing this disaster as it happened thousands of miles away, but you were able to feel its consequences, whether it was the ecological damage you were seeing on the television in front of you or the economic damage that you felt in your pocketbook from the gasoline prices that were sure to increase.

Definition of the Situation

Members of society are involved in a constant interaction with their environment, making choices in response to changing stimuli. This pattern of behavior is based on an individual interaction with one's cultural environment and is not an example of collective behavior. Collective behavior is the study of group behavior. As sociologists who study collective behavior, we are interested in individuals who suddenly find themselves trying to understand what is happening and how they respond to the effect of an unexpected event. We are specifically interested in identifying what people do when their routine world is unexpectedly disrupted.

When we use the term *unexpected events,* we are working on the assumption that people are suddenly exposed to a nonroutine event that causes disruption in their surrounding social order. We are interested in the behaviors and social processes that emerge when the former routine does not satisfy the new social needs of the situation. What more can we say about the structure or nature of unexpected events?

First of all, these events can all be regarded as some kind of crisis. These kinds of crises can be classified in terms of a scale based on the severity of impact on the society. At the most severe end of the scale is a disaster crisis, which involves large societies and large-scale physical harm. There is a severe disruption to the routine of everyday life, and new rules and social processes must be coordinated and negotiated by those involved in the disaster. On the other hand, an emergency crisis is defined as a situation in which traditional and existing social processes in place are strong enough to deal with the challenges and problems presented by the crisis. Another kind of crisis is one that may not produce a large number of victims and casualties but does cause an entire group to question its social values and processes. The social response to the death of Princess Diana and the public discussion that centered on the role of the monarchy in English society is an example of a social crisis.

As a sociologist, you have the expertise to identify the types of crises observable in society. Your analytical skills will teach you how to assess how members of society adapt to disruptions in their normal routine. As a result of your observations and analysis, you will understand that being able to identify the social behavior and processes that take place during apparently chaotic situations is a useful skill. As you will see, when we discuss research skills that you will need to study collective behavior, you will be able to use your skills to study phenomena that are unpredictable, unexpected, and subject to change, and that have no clear boundaries and little chance of dealing with objective subjects.

⧉ Why Do We Need to Make Sense of Unexpected Events?

How does the study of unexpected events help people in society? As students of collective behavior, we need to consider numerous levels of analysis. We need to understand how people perceive and cope with their lives when their surrounding social environment is thrown into chaos by an unexpected event. How does society deal with these challenges? The study of collective behavior provides the sociologist with the skills necessary to analyze complex societal challenges and crises.

At the same time, studying collective behavior gives an applied sociologist an arena in which to hone his or her skills. Given that we live in the world of instant news and overwhelming amounts of information, the ability to verify the accuracy of information is more important than ever. We need to be able to identify key factors in the information and come up with a meaningful and actionable interpretation. This analysis requires a concise but in-depth investigation of the factors leading to the occurrence, the activities associated with individuals and groups responding to the unexpected event, the consequences of the event, and the impact that the event will have on the individuals and community in the future. These "lessons learned" must then be shared with key leaders so that norms are created that will help others to deal with similar events in the future.

This is the major reason why sociologists need to make sense out of the unexpected. As applied sociologists, we want to help others anticipate and prepare for emergencies and disasters. We want to be able to show that even in unexpected situations, expected patterns of behavior will occur. This will help groups such as emergency management teams to develop plans that will maintain order during the event and minimize damage to both people and property.

Finally, the most important reason for making sense out of unexpected events is the ability to take diverse bodies of information and develop actionable intelligence that will enable individuals to spot conditions that may lead to crises or emergencies and resolve the problems before the event actually occurs. By doing so, you are able to take much of the "un" out of "unexpected."

⦿ Conceptualizing Unexpected Events

We have deliberately chosen the term *unexpected events* to allow us to observe those events that do not fit the formal definition of disaster. The formal definition of disaster points to the fulfillment of criteria that include large societies and evidence of large-scale physical harm. Wenger (1978) uses the terms *emergency* and *crisis* to classify and analyze disasters. An emergency is defined as a situation in which traditional and existing social processes are able to overcome the challenge and problems presented by the disaster. An emergency such as the sudden appearance of 15 inches of snow can be handled by a city in the snow belt. The mechanisms, group norms, and ways of proceeding with plans are established and can be put in place. Move the snowstorm to Florida, and we may now have a crisis. A crisis is a situation in which new social processes have to be established to overcome the problems presented by the disaster. There is an urgent need for otherwise obvious staples, such as snow-plows, winter coats, care for the homeless, people stranded in their cars on interstate highways, the ensuing strain on resources, and low blood transfusion supplies.

The concept of *time* is important in categorizing the social behavior that preceded or followed the occurrence of an unexpected event. Typically, time is studied as it relates to the event, such as the length of time that preceded the event and the length of time of any forewarning, the duration of the actual event, and the duration of the ensuing impact of the event. Time also becomes an important consideration when reviewing the amount of time it took emergency personnel to reach the scene and problems that these personnel may have had to overcome. The length of time that it takes for the social order to return to normal, routine activities can also be considered a measure of the impact of the unexpected event.

The concept of the *space* in which an event takes place is another important consideration in any analysis of the impact of unexpected events. For example, if people are trapped in an area with poor lighting, locked doors, and narrow corridors, such as a night club, the inclination to panic and fight to exit the building may be greater than if an emergency arises in a well-lit, well-organized space designed to facilitate an orderly exit, as in a modern sports stadium.

The *cultural environment* in which the incident occurs also must be taken into consideration. An understanding of the culture in which the unexpected events take place gives added value to the interpretation of the behavior displayed in a society disrupted by a disaster or an emergency. What is interesting to identify is whether the dominant culture is able to cope with the disruption of the new situation and hasten the return of the social order to its normal routine. Sometimes, the disruption will be too severe for the maintenance of the social order, leading to the emergence of new cultural norms and processes (Marx & McAdam, 1994). In a comparison of reactions by members of different cultures, do not assume that your value system holds true for other cultures. For example, Americans have an unconscious normative tendency to form orderly lines in order to gain access to large facilities. Europeans, on the other hand, are much more likely not to participate in the "queue" norm, instead pushing, shoving, and line-hopping their way to the front of any given line.

One of the most important means of communication, but also one of the most disturbing factors, that can emerge during a period of unstructured, nonroutine activities, such as that following a disaster or emergency, is the rumor. Rumors are defined as unreliable stories that have no identifiable source and are passed haphazardly from one person to another (Miller, 1985, p. 76). What actually happens is that during a period in which routine life is suspended, people want information to help them interpret their situation and make decisions about what to do next. Official information, which is often tightly controlled or may be unavailable, forces people to find other sources of information. Word of mouth messages and bits and pieces of information become molded into a seemingly credible story line. This process is the way that people make sense of the unstructured, nonroutine situation to increase a sense of personal control over their situation. However, the information is often inaccurate and may cause additional problems as people react to the incorrect information.

Panic is another concept that sociologists use to assess the social behavior following the occurrence of an unexpected event. The interest in the concept of panic is whether or not people, when faced with an impending disaster, will abandon any concern for others and demonstrate concern only for self-preservation. Most of the research says that during disasters, emergencies, or crises, people are more likely to display an altruistic concern for others and work with them to maintain some degree of composure. In recent years, disaster researchers have dedicated a large part of their studies to systematically gathering data on how groups react to a crisis. One of the consistent findings has been the small number of instances where large numbers of people have fled the scene in panic. It is very difficult to conceptualize an entire community fleeing the scene of a disaster or emergency. Actually, the opposite scenario—that of trying to persuade people to leave their homes—is more likely to occur.

It is important to point out that the initial narrative data on the event will usually be tainted by a media report of the event that leans toward an anecdotal description of people fleeing the scene in a very excited state. Normally, a sequential analysis of newspaper reports over the period during and after the actual event will show that the evacuation from the scene was relatively organized and coordinated.

One of the first things you want to look at is how people assemble preceding, during, and in response to a disruption to their perceived social order. The concept of assembling is a key ingredient in understanding social behavior in unexpected events. If we are looking at the aftermath of a disaster or emergency that occurred at a social event (such as a rock concert), then the process of assembling is an integral part of the investigation. Focus your attention on the kinds of instructions that people receive and the process that people use to converge or come together at the scene. Using the different cues from the surrounding environment, such as sirens, lights, news broadcasts, smells, and other noises, people get messages that something is happening, and many are known to converge at the scene of the emergency or disaster. This convergence at the scene of a disaster or emergency causes a lot of concern and usually leads to the standard process of erecting barriers to prevent unnecessary traffic in and around the scene, stop people from assembling in areas that might block access for emergency vehicles, or detour looters or curious sightseers from direct access to the scene.

When a crowd is already present at the scene of an emergency or disaster, the concept of *evacuation* comes into play. In the normal routine of attending a collective event, such as a baseball game or an indoor basketball game, there is a recognized emergency exit routine that can be activated as necessary. Research has shown that, in general, people will follow instructions and evacuate in the direction of the marked emergency exits (McPhail & Wohlstein, 1983). However, there are some situations in which it is impossible to follow an orderly evacuation because there may be a number of insurmountable barriers to following the normal evacuation instructions (e.g., fire, smoke, toxic fumes, water flowing uncontrollably, narrow doors, narrow hallways, inoperative emergency systems, and difficulty in hearing instructions). Situations like these are conducive to a stampede, often with fatal results.

Another evacuation process involves the need to evacuate an entire community due to a major threat, such as a spill or chemical leak in the vicinity. This type of evacuation process is difficult to achieve and may, in some cases, require the unusual act of arresting residents and removing them by force from the area. Many residents refuse to leave their homes in order to protect their property, and others stay to be with their pets. The speed with which the social control forces, police, security guards, or military are able to reach the scene and the methods used to secure the area are key, and the sociologist will want to analyze them when assessing the situation.

Following the aftermath of the incident, a cultural process *assigning blame for the event* is sometimes observed. Questions are posed to ascertain whether the incident could have been avoided, the extent of the damage incurred, and the identification of those who may be responsible. Optimistically, one hopes that the reason for proceeding with this process is to establish preventive measures to ensure that this does not happen again. One of the unfortunate effects of the Oklahoma City bombing is the distinct future threat of terrorist activity in this country. Because this is not a normal experience for most Americans, it is to be expected that it will take some time to convince people of the reality of the threat. The publicity and coverage that ensues from the investigation of such a disaster may serve to inform people of future dangers and raise awareness when informed of any future threats.

As sociologists who study social behavior in the context of unexpected events, we are interested in what these experiences mean to people and how they interpret these disruptive situations. As we have noted elsewhere, despite the complex academic models established to provide definitions of disasters, people may establish their own criteria for disasters as they define and respond to events in their surroundings. The knowledge and understanding of the numerous theoretical perspectives is one of the most important skills you will need in order to make sense out of unexpected situations. First, one of the oldest theories in use, *social contagion* (Gustave LeBon, 1879), maintains that people react to nonroutine disruptions to their lives with hysterical outbursts and behavior that is out of control. This behavior erupts because of intense stressful feelings that are rapidly communicated in a gathered group of people. Once this hysteria has calmed down, social order will return. This perspective becomes apparent when we hear reports of panicked people fleeing burning buildings and planes.

In complete contrast, the *emergent norm* perspective (Turner & Killian, 1957) says that routine responses to social behavior are suspended and become unclear when the individuals are exposed to a major societal disruption. As a result, people develop emerging or new norms and processes to deal with the situations. The creation of temporary groups and changes in role definitions and relationships are typically a part of these emerging responses.

The *social behavioral/interactionist theory* (McPhail & Miller, 1973) is used to look at the processes involved in the movement of people in and out of areas during an emergency or disruptive event. Here, we find a comprehensive body of literature and examples of how to observe, identify, and record collective behavior while it is happening or after it has happened. This is a perspective that focuses on the action of gathering data to conduct analysis on the concepts of assembly and dispersal. McPhail and Miller maintain that social behavior in a disruptive arena occurs as the result of messages on how to gather, disperse, or evacuate and is perceived as the result of an interaction between members of a social group.

The *value-added perspective* (Smelser, 1962) posits the view that people behave in a certain way in response to a perceived threat to their situation. Analysis of social behavior using this perspective is based on locating the behavior within a certain context, such as a panic, craze, disaster, protest march, or revolution. This perspective examines the entire context, motivations, and activities that occur during the disruption and then evaluates the response of social control forces in bringing the situation under control.

As with most theoretical perspectives, there is no one completely accurate theory to use with all collective behavior events. This is why it is important for the analyst to be aware of the use of each of the perspectives as they fit the situation. Therefore, the researcher will need to use a number of ex post facto (i.e., after the fact) research techniques in order to analyze the event and its ramifications.

▧ Research Tools

We have already indicated that it is usually difficult to be present at an unexpected event. The use of the case study is regarded as an appropriate research design for investigating the social behavior associated with unexpected events. However, it is strongly recommended that the case study method use a multimethod triangulation approach. For example, there are at least five easily identifiable sources of data that can be gathered to make sense of unexpected events. These data sources include visits to the site of the event; personal interviews with different actors; a content analysis of newspaper accounts; an evaluation of photographs and television broadcasts; and a comprehensive review of official documents, such as police reports, disaster reports, or the findings of official inquiries. In addition to those sources mentioned, the addition of data provided by CNN and MSNBC's 24-hour global news coverage are powerful new sources of information for your analysis.

Site Visits

As soon as possible after the event, it is important to visit the site. This should be done both when the site is empty and also when postevent activities are going on. Visiting the empty site allows the investigator to view the physical environment surrounding the occurrence, the parameters of the area, the physical barriers already present without the activity or crowd, the advantages and disadvantages of the structure of the area, the exits, the overall pattern of the structure as an arena in which the event took place, the height and breadth of the area, and the accessibility of the avenues for escape and/or rescue present in the area. On the other hand, visiting the site or a similar site when there is a full crowd allows the researcher to identify the demographics of the crowd present, those who might prefer to sit or stand in one area over another, the noise level of the crowd, and the manner in which social control was maintained. An understanding of the particular culture of the context you are investigating is an advantage and will add richness to your event analysis or narrative.

Personal Interviews

Personal interviews are considered excellent sources for studying details surrounding the factors that contributed to the unexpected events. Interviews can be conducted with such personnel as police officers, community leaders, local government representatives, emergency personnel, and any other individual or organization representative who might be in a position to provide information. Prepare an agenda of questions based on the information you have gained from newspaper reports and television broadcasts. You may find that once you start interviewing a person, the information flows in such a way that you do not need to ask specific questions. In any case, make sure that you tape (with permission) each interview and/or take very thorough notes.

Newspaper Accounts

Although newspaper reports are useful for providing accounts of the activities surrounding the event, there are some difficulties in using newspaper data. First, journalists prepare stories for publishing and send them forward to the editor for approval. In many cases, stories are edited and cut to fit the space available. Cantor, Comber, and Uzzel (1989) point out that newspapers have one inherent flaw: They only ask a few people for their views, and the questions have a habit of determining the answers received. In addition, newspapers are likely to select only the answers that fit the story line being presented (Cantor et al., 1989, p. 4). Also, when narrating the activities of a group, journalists are more likely to deal with a unit of behavior, which makes little allowance for the presence of different groups and meanings within the event.

The most appropriate method of analyzing information from the newspapers is to gather data from an entire sequence of stories as a unit of data rather than relying on the data provided in a single story (Danzger, 1975, p. 576). Data from newspapers can be used in a variety of ways. First, a sequential narrative of the event can be compiled from a number of different publications. Second, demographic information can be obtained about the participants; the victims, if any; the injured; and the survivors' families. Third, data from the newspapers can be used to identify the differences in the actions and reactions of different actors and roles as a result of the unexpected event. Finally, data gathered from the newspapers can provide an initial indication of the potential for new emerging social roles and processes.

Photographs and Broadcast News

Photographs play an important part in this type of study for a number of reasons. First, photographs capture the emotion of the moment, and the examination of photographs following a collective episode can give the researcher a sense of emotion and intent of the participants. Think about the societal response to the death of Princess Diana. The photographs of the many tributes and shrines erected gave us a glimpse of the depth of feeling being demonstrated in London and Paris. Photographs provide evidence of the depth of space, and whether they are dense or light in cover is important in identifying the type of behavior and demographics of the participants. Photographs can also be made to provide a display of public emotion over time during and following the period of the disaster.

As a result of the growth and development of global communications technology, our ability to gather data and be armchair participant observers of events as they unfold in many areas of the world is greatly enhanced by the advent of 24-hour global cable news coverage. In the absence of an ability to conduct a site visit, the 24-hour cable coverage system has served to make the world smaller and brings an added bonus to our data collection efforts.

Official Documents

As is customary following a disaster such as the Murrah building explosion, the death of Princess Diana, or the crash of TWA flight 800 to Paris, an official inquiry is launched to investigate the cause and make recommendations for the prevention of a future occurrence. The official inquiry contributes to the process of providing an objective, rational explanation for what happened, why it happened, and how to prevent it from happening again. Examples of such documents are police reports, police files, emergency personnel reports, and the proceedings of official government inquiries. These documents are usually made available to the public and typically can be obtained from the investigating agency or over the Internet.

▧ Presentation Tools

The major problem you face when making a presentation is the overwhelming amount of information that you will have gathered during the investigation. We encourage you to gather as much information as possible in order to provide yourself with a rich database upon which to base your findings. Now, you need to report these findings in a way that focuses on brevity and conciseness. First of all, you may need to prepare a series of different reports that are designed for different audiences. Depending on the type of event that you have chosen for your study, your audiences may run the gamut from the general public to an official government agency or board of inquiry. If at all possible, prepare a multimedia presentation that can be used routinely with boilerplate text that has been adapted for your target audience. The use of summative overhead text, selected photographs, storyboards, video clips, and any props or artifacts from the event are powerful motivators for the audience to focus on your presentation.

One suggested approach is to construct a report based on a chronology of the event. Make a brief, concise presentation that focuses on providing answers to the main issues of interest to your audience. Prepare additional information in a multimedia format that will enable you to answer additional questions on areas that might be of interest to the audience. Remember, you have assumed the role of expert in presenting these data to the audience, and you have more expertise than you probably thought you had. So be prepared to think on your feet!

Most importantly, listen carefully to the questions you are asked, because they may provide you with a richer understanding of the data you have analyzed.

▧ Sociologist as Expert

As a researcher interested in making sense out of unexpected events, you will have the knowledge of the tools and skills needed to conduct a multimethod analysis of the collective action. The dynamic nature of an event requires the use of a combination of data collection techniques and an awareness of the flaws and strengths of the data that may be reported as a result of these data collection tools. Also, as an analyst, you are the medium through which others can come to an understanding of the social patterns of behavior that emerge or surround the event under investigation. You bear the responsibility of presenting data in an objective, balanced manner but also maintaining a gestalt awareness of the nature of the event. This is a skill that is gained through empirical experience and openness to new perspectives.

Sociologists are uniquely qualified to analyze unexpected events. We are trained to identify how people act in "normal" situations, and we have both the theoretical and methodological knowledge to understand the difference between routine and unexpected social events. Most importantly, we have been trained to view all social behavior as important. Our sociological curiosity will lead us into using a broad-brush analysis of the event in order to define it, understand it, explain it, and possibly set up criteria that will allow others to better deal with a similar problem in the future.

▧ Case Study

The Case

A fire broke out at a St. Valentine's Day dance in a small metropolitan city nightclub. The nightclub was located on the third floor of the building. More than 200 people paid to attend the event in an entertainment area designed to hold 150 people. Initial media reports indicate that people ran screaming from the building, and that there was a stampede. A tossed cigarette is alleged to have started the fire. More than 48 people died in this fire, and more than 150 others escaped. All of the victims were under the age of 21. The band continued to play in order to assist with an orderly evacuation out of the building. Three members of the band are still unaccounted for. Many of the victims were found lying on top of each other at three of the fire exits. An unconfirmed news report states that, with the exception of the main entrance, all other exit doors were padlocked shut. Many of the bystanders who have gathered at the scene early this morning said that this was "an accident waiting to happen."

As a sociologist, you have been asked to join a team of investigators to identify the causes and assess the conditions, the event catalyst, and the postevent behaviors of the personnel surrounding the event. In addition, you are asked to provide a preliminary report on the person or people who may be responsible for this disaster and make any recommendations you see fit to protect the lives of other nightclub clients in the city. Your committee has 3 weeks to produce a preliminary report. At your first meeting, the mayor emphasized the need for quick findings, recommendations, and action. How would you handle this project?

Possible Solutions

Here are a number of suggested solutions to the above problem. Each situation requires the overall use of skills and knowledge that you have gained during your studies. It is strongly recommended that you use a multimethod approach.

Political Reality of the Situation

First of all, recognize that you are in the middle of a politically sensitive issue, and although the political pressures of the day may seem great, your first responsibility is to provide the committee with your best effort to find answers to the questions presented to you. This means that you may not be able to provide a full report by the date requested. Provide a report that details the progress you have made to date based on the use of sound research techniques and skills.

Full Access to Data Collection

1. Work with the committee to establish a time line of tasks that need to be completed. This is a good way to highlight the amount of work that needs to be done and identify those tasks that can be completed easily.

2. Establish a research methodology for the systematic gathering of data necessary to provide a narrative of the event and respond to the questions asked.

3. Make a list of data that need to be gathered. For example, inquest reports on the victims, news video recordings, police reports, official comments, building inspections, building code violations, safety systems in place in the building, taped interviews, newspaper reports, survivor accounts of the event, emergency personnel reports, and any other reports of similar accidents and the findings of subsequent investigations.

Data Analysis

Once the data have started to come in to the committee, immediately organize and analyze what you have. Work with the committee members to divide up the analysis of the incident by area of expertise. There are endless options for analysis. Some possible divisions of analysis might be as follows:

1. A narrative of the events as they occurred over time. For example, before the event, during the event, the aftermath of the event, and other findings as they became available in the days following the disaster.

2. A description of the injuries sustained by the victims and their location at the scene.

3. A description of the history of the building in which the incident took place. Details should include the name of the owner, the safety record, the age and structure of the building, the layout of the scene, and any other details that may come to light during the investigation.

4. A narrative of the process followed by survivors as they exited the building. Use a graph or diagram to augment the narrative.

5. A report on the findings that emerged from interviews with various individuals who had any contact with the scene.

Report Preparation

1. Prepare brief reports by sections on areas targeted for analysis. Use graphs to illustrate the relationships and activities that are pertinent to the understanding of the specific report.

2. Bring in experts in the areas targeted for analysis to support the findings of the committee. You will not only be presenting a report, but you will also be starting on the task of making recommendations for preventing future occurrences.

Policy Recommendations

Make recommendations based on your best evaluation of what needs to be done to prevent a future occurrence. The inclusion of a budget cost associated with the implementation of this recommendation is strongly advised.

▧ Exercises

The interesting aspect of making sense out of unexpected events is that the only way to study an event fully is as it is happening in its own theater. We have tried to develop a series of exercises to help you understand better how to study these events. These exercises make use of basic research tools such as content analysis, interviewing skills, and the review of photographs and official documents. You might even be able to find information on the World Wide Web.

1. Locate and read news media accounts of two natural disasters, one that occurred 20 years ago and one that occurred within the past 5 years. The disasters should be of a similar nature (e.g., news reports dealing with ecological disasters such as oil spills or similar weather disasters such as hurricanes). If possible, build a chronology of time and space as it relates to the event from the reports of both events. What do you think? Is reporting more detailed now or 20 years ago? Compare the news reports dealing with both disasters. What are the similarities and the differences? Identify the prioritization of information as identified by the media in their reports. What would you have liked to see that was omitted from the stories?

2. Find people in your community who have participated either as official representatives of an emergency management team or as volunteers who converged on the scene of a disaster to give assistance. Ask them to describe their experiences. You will need to use an informal personal interviewing strategy. (Remember to ask permission to record responses, and ask the respondents to sign a waiver to protect their rights to give permission for the publication of any of their responses.) Ask questions that deal with issues such as their motive for involvement in such activities; the sorts of activities in which they participated; whether they accomplished their perceived goals; and what else they thought needed to be done. If possible, try to gather information from the official emergency management representatives about their atti-

tudes toward and opinions of the participation of emergent volunteers during the disaster.

3. Call your county emergency management representative and seek an informational interview. Your assignment is to identify the greatest threats to a community and how emergency management personnel make use of sociological skills and concepts to prepare the community for impending disasters, such as hurricanes or floods.

4. Identify a recent unexpected event that can be classified as a social crisis. Document the social response and process of dealing with the impact of the social crisis and how the members of the community or society returned to normal life. Identify new processes and social rituals that emerged during this crisis.

5. Suppose you work as the director of public relations for a local hospital. Your job is to promote the services and image of the hospital and to be prepared to deal with threats to that image. You are called into an emergency meeting of top hospital officials, who request that you prepare a press release outlining the fact that a hospital doctor who has worked in the emergency room for the past 3 years has been confirmed as a carrier of the AIDS virus. The hospital *might* have a potential crisis on its hands. Social reactions to a situation like this bring into play such sociological concepts as rumor, panic, and mass hysteria. How would you deal with a situation like this?

Responding to Demographic Challenges: Applied Sociology

Although most introductory texts in sociology have a section on demography, it is rare that demographics gets integrated into the applied or basic sociological mixture. This is unfortunate because demography, the study of human population, is such a critical ingredient in applied sociology. In this chapter, we will provide an overview of the basic ideas behind demography. Then, we will examine the value of demography in a variety of settings that can be addressed by applied sociologists. In the tools section, we will introduce you to the basic formulas for calculating key demographic measures.

⬛ Applying a Demographic Perspective

When we think of demography, we often "think big!" This is often a macrolevel idea. We are usually talking about societies, how their populations grow, and how many people are living in the society. For applied sociologists, this is a valid beginning and an important one. We need to know the dynamics of these population "social facts." Whether we like it or not, people are born, they die, and they move in and out of social systems. Because this is a macro phenomenon, we might not notice the changes that demographic facts make immediately. Demographic factors need to be viewed at other levels for their direct and indirect population effects in all social interactions.

In addition, we need to think about demographic factors as more than just a bunch of numbers. When we say that the People's Republic of China has more than one billion people living within its borders, it is more than just the number 1,000,000,000+. Remember that every one of those people has biological, personal, and social needs. The idea of "one billion" is staggering. It is difficult for us to even imagine one billion of anything. Yet here we are saying that one billion people share a commonly socially defined reality called "China." They eat, sleep, work, have fun, have kids, and die like other people. Although there are in excess of one billion individual people, one billion sets of individual needs, we realize the presence and value of social systems that must support this mass of humanity. Without a complex social structure and complex supporting systems of norms and values to shore up this group of people, it would be obvious that this huge applied problem could not be solved.

We could have just as easily used the United States as an example. The numbers (260,000,000+) and geopolitical conditions would change, but the idea would be the same. The key concept here is that population has little meaning unless it is viewed in terms of social demography. By this we mean the interplay between population factors and social systems. We are challenged to ask many questions in light of changing population factors. For example, how does sheer increase in total population affect the way we organize our lives? What other factors simultaneously influence social systems and population to produce changes in human patterns? Let us jump to the other end of the social organizational system, the micro level, for another example that may "bring this idea home."

Microlevel impacts are likely to be obvious; we just need to think of them in demographic terms. Take the all-important decision to bring a child into the world. We can envision this as a demographic problem at a variety of levels. We can view this at a macro level ("What is the number of children born in the United States on any given day?"), at a meso level ("What is the number of children born in our county on a given day?"), or at a micro level ("What is the number of children born in this family on a given day?"). At this point, all of these questions reflect only the numbers. But let us consider the questions in terms of impact; in other words, what impact will the presence of these children have on the way we live our lives at each level? To focus clearly on this event, let us see what happens at the micro level.

Suppose we envision a woman and a man in their early 20s and, for the sake of discussion, imagine that they are married to one another. These two people live together in a one-bedroom apartment in an urban setting in the United States. They are both currently employed and they are both college-educated. She is a nurse at a local hospital, and he is a financial representative for a local bank. They decide that they want to have a baby. She becomes pregnant. What is the social demographic impact on this social setting?

We might do well to return to the use of structural-functionalist tools. First of all, what is the current setting? Our couple lives in a dyad, a two-person group. The very structure of a two-person group versus a three-person group (a triad) has long been known to social scientists. In Georg Simmel's (1902) classic work on group size, he explains the changes that occur simply by adding one person to the group. Triads make it possible for multiple structures to emerge that are not possible within the dyad. Relationships may form between any combination of two people in the triad: Mom-baby, Dad-baby, and Mom-Dad are all possibilities. Triads produce increased complexity. So if, at the end of a normal gestation period, one child is born, a social transition will occur, and as a result of the transition, the population in the household will represent a natural increase of 1, which is a rate of natural increase of 50%. This is just the first impact. We have not even begun to explore other elements in the social system. From a functionalist view, this produces disequilibrium in the social system. As you recall, disequilibrium will take the form of deviance and then change.

Now, let us look at the impact of other factors on this relationship. We now expect three people to live in the same space in which two lived before. The density of the population increases. That is, the number of square feet per person decreases. The amount of available living space that each person has becomes smaller. Other resources are also influenced. Cribs, diapers, and baby clothes are only the beginning of a list of resources necessary to support this change. The impact of internal and external economic factors needs to be addressed. Wages earned by our couple must now be extended to cover the needs of three instead of two. Of course, this presupposes that both parents will continue to work after a short maternity leave for Mom, which simply may not be the case. Who will take care of the baby? Our couple will need to decide whether they will rely on external sources of care (other family members, paid care providers, or both) and/or whether they will respond to the child's need for care by individually or collectively withdrawing from their work roles. Regardless of how this is determined, the outcome is not without economic impact. More resources are used at some cost to the family's social and economic systems. Economic factors are only one of many organizational factors that need attention. If our couple is representative of a nuclear family in the United States, the residual effects of these changes will be borne largely by the micro relationship between them. The impact on the self of changing social roles and statuses (becoming a mother, becoming a father); role confusion and conflict (stay a wage earner, stay a parent, or do both); and role strain (e.g., playing the role of parent by taking the 2 a.m. feedings, changing the unexpected messy diapers) will all "wash up" on the shores of the relationship between these two.

Extended family relationships can absorb some of this impact by sharing resources and providing child care if these (time and other resources) are available and if the willingness to provide them is also available. Day care and child development centers may also provide necessary support. Families that are neolocal (move to a place away from their extended family or family of origin) will find these options narrowed. Government and health care systems will be directly affected. A birth certificate will be issued and become part of an expanding archive of social data. The local hospital and the medical systems on-line before, during, and after the child's birth will all be influenced. Religious systems likewise will be involved to a greater or lesser degree in this phenomenon.

This impact on social systems is still only a portion of the effect of this microlevel population change. The presence of the child not only means more resources used but also more waste. The by-products of living produce an impact on the environment. We already mentioned the impact on crowding in the household, but do not forget the plastic diapers, empty baby food containers, and other related items that end up in sewage systems and landfills, along with unexpected noise and asynchronous schedules that affect the social and natural environments. Modern child care is enhanced by a variety of technologies. Baby formula, disposable diapers, electronic monitoring devices, not to mention a variety of child educational devices are just some of the direct technological forces used in the care of the child. The technology that perhaps has a greater effect is the presence of a wide range of easily obtainable birth control devices and procedures that predated this child's entrance into the world.

Our intent is not to frighten you out of having children (or, if you have them, make you think that you have committed some kind of crime)—far from it. Our intent is simply to personalize this situation somewhat. We want you to be aware of at least two things. First, demographic factors can have an impact at macro, meso, and micro levels. Thinking at each level is valuable in understanding the effects of population changes beyond the numbers. Second, we want to show the importance of social demography. Population changes always are interpreted in light of at least three other factors: organization, environment, and technology. As the famous social ecologist Amos Hawley (1971) pointed out, we can think in terms of POET (population, organization, environment, and technology) when we think of interacting social factors.

░ The Balancing Equation

An important skill that any social scientist should have (particularly an applied sociologist) is the ability to measure dimensions and change in human populations. Do not get too nervous here! Yes, we are talking about math, but not difficult math. Demographers are some of the most mathematical of sociologists. Truly, a person may spend his or her entire life researching human population, and good demography is a challenge. However, you can provide good basic analysis of an applied situation with some basic tools. You need to know three things: (a) what you plan to measure; (b) how to measure it; and (c) where to get the data (if, of course, you are not doing primary research). In this section, we will work our way through the measurement tools necessary to address a number of important demographic forces.

First, let us look at the basic balancing equation, as the Population Reference Bureau calls it (see Figure 10.1). If you think about it for a minute, the basic population equation is made up of a straightforward approach. First, there is a target area. This could be a place or perhaps an organization. This could be the state of New Jersey, for example, or it could be General Motors Corporation. Now, determine how many people live there (count by way of a census or, if necessary, an estimate). That is the population at a starting point. To figure out what the population is now, add the things that will increase population (i.e., births and people moving into the area). Subtract from this equation the things that decrease population (i.e., death and people moving out of the area). That will give you the new population. So, our first and overarching population equation, the "balancing equation," is the following:

P(Time 1) + Births − Deaths +/− migration = P(Time 2)

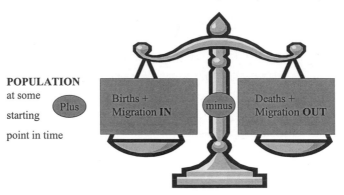

Figure 10.1 The Population Balancing Equation for a Defined Place

That is all there is to it! Although we can accomplish a great deal with this equation, we need to remember that populations are very complex. For example, let us borrow data from the U.S. Census. The Census estimates the population of the United States by using an equation that predicts the elements of the balancing equation over time! In this way, the Census provides us with a population clock, but it is really nothing more than an application of the previous equation. On December 12, 1996, we read the population clock at two points in time—9:16:14 a.m. and 9:17:04 a.m.—which is 50 seconds apart. The clock was set this way:

One birth every	8 seconds
One death every	13 seconds
One international migrant (net) every	43 seconds
One federal U.S. citizen (net) returning every	4,108 seconds
Net gain of one person every	15 seconds

At 9:16:14 a.m. on December 12, 1996, the estimated population of the United States was 266,269,184. Using the clock settings for the elements of the balancing equation, we would estimate the following 50 seconds later:

		Calculated	Rounded
Births	50/8	6.25	6
Deaths	50/13	–3.85	–4
International migrants (net)	50/43	1.16	1
Federal U.S. citizens (net) returning	50/4,108	0.01	0
Net gain		3.57	3

The Census clock uses rounded figures, so we would use our formula as follows: Population when you start + Births – Deaths +/– Migration = New population or 266,269,184 + 6 – 4 + 1 = 266,269,187.

When we checked the Census population clock at 9:17:04 a.m. on December 12, 1996, the estimated population of the United States was 266,269,187.

📓 Age and Sex

Demographers, and therefore applied sociologists, pay close attention to the age composition and sex (gender) composition of a population. The reasons are pretty clear. If you remember the balancing equation discussed above, age and gender have a great deal to do with birth and death, two of the major elements in the population balancing equation. Because incoming population depends in part on the number of births in a society, it makes sense that we need to know how many people (i.e., women) are able to give birth. But not just any women; we are concerned with the number of women who are of childbearing age. Although the tabloid papers we read standing in line at the grocery store have cover stories on the 6-year-old girl or the 87-year-old woman who has given birth, in general, the age range for women who can give birth (women who are fecund) is 15 to 44 years old.

Now, let us put the sex and age characteristics together. Demographers need to be concerned with the number of women in a population who are between 15 and 44 years of age. This gives them an idea of the potential fertility in a society. Hence, we get a sense of the number of births that will be added to a population. Of course, it is not just a matter of age and sex that sets the potential level of fertility. We also need to apply other social factors in this thinking. Attitudes toward fertility, motherhood, social class, knowledge of birth control and family planning, religious attitudes, as well as attitudes toward work in the economic sector of society are just some of the forces that influence actual numbers of births.

Now you can see why we need more than one way to measure fertility. Sometimes, births are expressed as the number of births divided by the total population. This is called the *crude birthrate*—and crude it is! As you can see, this calculation can hide reality. The number of births is clear enough, but what about the total population? This includes all the people who can give birth (15- to 44-year-old women), and a large number of people who cannot give birth (everybody else, including men)! This number is a reasonable starting point, but using it exclusively could produce surprises. If we think about it, we need an equation that reflects the total number of births with the number of people who are able to give birth. How about if we divide the number of births by the number of women between the ages of 15 and 44? This is called the *general fertility rate.*

Using data from the National Center for Health Statistics (Ventura, Martin, Curtain, & Mathews, 1977), suppose we wish to compare fertility by racial group in the United States. Here is what we would find for 1994:

	All Races	White	Black	American Indian	Asian or Pacific Islander
Crude birthrate (per 1,000)	15.2	14.4	19.5	17.1	17.5
General fertility rate (per 1,000)	66.7	64.9	76.9	70.9	66.8

Notice how the general fertility rate gives us a better picture of the actual fertility situation in a target area (a country, a county, a city, etc.)? We can make better comparisons between areas because this equation standardizes the numbers we are comparing. Actually, the general fertility rate is a specific example of an age-specific rate. You can compare the number of births in an age-group of women with the number of women in that age-group. Our equation would then be the number of births in an age-group of women divided by the number of women in that same age-group. This is called the *age-specific fertility rate.* For example, suppose we were concerned about young women having children prior to graduation from high school. We could calculate the fertility rate for the 15- to 17-year-old age-group by dividing the number of births in that age-group by the number of young women in the same group. Multiplying this result by a constant in order to make it a percentage would give a specific rate of women in that age-group having children.

Now, let us turn to other age-related phenomena. The age composition of a population has a great deal to do with patterns of social action in a society. As you may have guessed after our discussion of birth, the impact of a younger population on a society could result in an increase in the number of children; and, therefore, an increase in a dependent population and all that goes with it: child care, parenting, and education, as well as childhood illnesses. The impact of an aging population likewise has an impact on what a target group does. Like children, elderly people make great personal and social contributions to society. However, with age comes an increase in physical deterioration, higher rates of morbidity, and eventually death (mortality).

Like fertility, death rates need to be used in more than one way to measure mortality. Deaths are expressed as the number of deaths divided by the total population. This is called the *crude death rate*. Once again, this calculation masks reality. The number of deaths is clear enough, but what about the total population? This includes all the people in a given population, and there may be specific groups that will have higher death rates than others. Again, this number is a reasonable start, but using it exclusively could produce surprises. How about if we divide the number of deaths in a given age-group by the total number of people in that target age-group? This is called the *age-specific death rate*. Another way to calculate death rates is to use a *cause-specific death rate*. With this type of death rate, the total number of deaths from a selected illness is divided by the total number of people in a given target population.

▨ Migration

People move in and out of an area, a target population, a county, a company, or a family. Let us reflect on our earlier example of a family and the demographic effects therein. Let us move our family down the familial developmental cycle toward midlife and beyond. What happens? The children grow up and migrate out of the house. They leave, for awhile at least, and join the military, go to college, get a job, or all of the above. Sometimes, they return to take up residence on a temporary basis. Eventually, they leave and set up their own homes and, perhaps, their own families.

At a micro level, we can see the effect of migration out (emigration) and migration in (immigration). When the children leave, parents may get the notion that they can convert resources formerly used by the kids to some other purpose. For example, that extra bedroom may become an office. There are fewer mouths to feed, at least directly, as well as less water used and less time and energy spent on the direct supervision of children. Midlife parents come to realize that their children's emigration is a process, not a single event. It takes place over time and rarely happens overnight!

Regardless of the time frame, this microlevel example gives us a sense of the social impact of migration. Planning for population movement in and out of a target social environment has critical impact on the demand for resources and social needs. This is one of the reasons that countries attempt to limit immigration. An increase in population due to births and deaths is often more easily estimated than is the addition of people due to migration. People will attempt to migrate, legal or not, if the cost of moving in is outweighed by the perceived benefit of the move. Demographers consider this in terms of "push" and "pull" forces. Push forces are factors that drive people out of an area. For example, political unrest or civil war may start a flood of refugees across international boundaries. The push factors need not be so blatant. Poor economic conditions (lack of jobs, lack of economic opportunity) and quality of life conditions (available health care and other social services) may also push people across the border. Similarly, pull forces may attract people into an area. Expanded job opportunities and the promise of a better life draw people to an area. People will take great risks and possibly engage in illegal behavior to improve their chances for a better life.

As a nation of immigrants, the United States has witnessed the impact of both the strengths and weaknesses associated with this sort of population movement. Waves of migration have washed ashore on U.S. soil. The collective worth of the diverse people who have migrated to the United States, their ideas and energy, have no doubt had a great impact on the emergence of the society as a 20th-century leader. On the other hand, unexpected or unplanned migration can tax the limits of social systems. Reflect on our microlevel example for a moment.

What happens when the midlife parents open the front door of their home to find their daughter and her three children arriving to take up residence because of some life crisis (death or divorce—push factors)?

This is a microlevel example, but we could see this as easily at the next level. What happens if the area in which you live becomes an attractive suburb for a major urban area? Many families show up at the county or city doorstep. They expect services, and they expect structural accommodations: schools, churches, shopping centers, and recreation facilities. Many local areas have invoked growth ordinances that make land developers responsible for providing sewage and water treatment facilities before building permits can be issued. In this way, growth can at least be planned to some degree. Real problems arise with growth for which there has been no planning and, hence, no infrastructure to support human social life. Migration must be accounted for when addressing an applied problem.

▧ Research Tools

Researching demographic factors can be complicated business. In most cases, however, we can get a start on the nature of a target population by asking three basic questions:

1. How many people are there?
2. What kind of people?
3. What is the nature of growth in this group?

Let us take these in turn. When we ask "How many?" we think about counting them, of course. Research in demography means counting! We must first determine the boundaries in which we plan to do the counting. Is it a country, a county, a community, a factory, or a family? We need to be clear about who should be included. These boundaries may be determined in at least time, space, and social identification. For example, we may want to count everyone who was born between 1947 and 1957 in the United States. This gives a time-geopolitical set of boundaries for our enumeration. This particular group, or cohort, has been labeled the "baby boomers." People in this group have been assigned a social categorization.

This approach could just as easily have been used at another level of social organization. Earlier in this chapter, we provided a vignette of a micro example: a family. Now let us move to the meso level. We could count the number of people who are working in the company in which you are employed or the college that you currently attend. In either case, we would need to set the boundaries for counting in time, space, and social identification. Let us extend this idea of social identification.

This is where we ask the second question: "What kind of people?" By this, we are concerned about the characteristics of the people we want to count. We have noted already the importance of age and sex to demographers. When we move into the realm of social demography, we need to investigate the ethnic and racial characteristics of our target population. This is important because cultural and social class distinctions in human populations can have a major impact on factors such as social organization and resource use. When people migrate into an area, they bring their culture, their way of life, with them. So, it is not sufficient to simply ask "How many?" Rather, we need to ask "How many and who?"

The final question in this brief view of demography is "What is the nature of growth in this group?" Anything that grows changes from moment to moment. The growth question is a potent one and is interwoven in the other two questions that preceded it. The rate of reproduction, the mortality rate, and the willingness to migrate will eventually try the limits of social structure. Rapid growth may outstrip a social system's ability to support it (leading to crowding, even starvation), whereas failure to grow may create comparable problems (e.g., labor shortages, reduction in tax revenues). Measuring growth, actual and potential, is critical in planning human social structures.

Now, we return to doing the counting. There are two major ways in which this is done. The first is an attempt to actually count everyone: a census. Counting everyone sounds simple, but it rarely is. The time and space factors we have mentioned, combined with other social identification issues (How do you count homeless people? Are people who are not citizens counted?), complicates counting. The second counting procedure is to mathematically estimate the number of people. Population estimates like the one we used in our example of the U.S. Bureau of the Census population clock are becoming increasingly accurate. In periods between government census counts each decade, the Bureau of the Census relies on this information. State, province, and local governments, as well as business, health care, and other community organizations, likewise use estimates to assess population growth and likely impact. As applied sociologists, we may need to rely on these estimates. Everyone need not have the extreme level of mathematical sophistication to create some of these complex models. However, basic equations that can be used to measure population dimensions are valuable. The equations provided by the Population Reference Bureau in Chart 10.1 are good basic research tools.

☒ Presentation Tools

Population information is graph-friendly! The number, kind, and growth levels of human population make great pictures, and we recommend that you always consider using a graphic presentation when you

Chart 10.1   Some Useful Population Equations

Birthrate = (Number of births/Total population) × a constant

General fertility rate = (Number of births/Number of births to women ages 15 to 44) × a constant

Death rate = (Number of deaths/Total population) × a constant

Infant mortality rate = (Number of deaths of infants under age 1/Total live births) × a constant

Immigration rate = (Number of people migrating in/Total population into which they are migrating) × a constant

Emigration rate = (Number of people migrating out/Total population from which they are migrating) × a constant

Incidence (sickness or other characteristic) rate = (Number of people developing a certain characteristic in a time period/Total population at risk) × a constant

Prevalence (sickness or other characteristic) rate = (Number of people with a certain characteristic in a time period/Total population at risk) × a constant

Natural increase = Births − Deaths

Rate of natural increase = [(Births in a given time frame − Deaths in the same time frame)/Total population] × a constant

Growth rate = [(Births in a given time frame − Deaths in the same time frame + or − Migration)/Total population] × a constant

Doubling time = 70/Growth rate expressed as a percentage

Sex ratio = (Number of males/Number of females) × a constant

Age-specific ratio = (Number of people with a certain characteristic in a certain age-group/Number of people in that age-group) × a constant

---

SOURCE: Adapted from Population Reference Bureau (1997).

are presenting these data. Become comfortable with a frequently available computer graphing or presentation package like Powerpoint, Harvard Graphics, or Corel. Present information in clear bar charts, curves, or pie charts. Do not get too fancy—avoid graphophrenia! Just because you can show eight colored curves on a graph does not mean that you should. Making a good transparency for overhead projection or conducting an electronic presentation are two good ways to show population data. A population pyramid is an example of a modified bar graph. In the population pyramid, age is expressed on the vertical axis (usually expressed in categories of age across the life span). On the horizontal axis, the number (or percentage) of men in each age category is presented on the left with the number (or percentage) of women on the right. The result resembles the shape of a pyramid. The power of graphic presentations becomes obvious as the distribution of an age cohort of people works its way through a society over time.

Where should you get the data for your presentation? If your target is a national population characteristic, you are probably in luck. The

U.S. Census Bureau and comparable bureaus in many countries support reasonably up-to-date population data. The United Nations, World Bank, and the Population Reference Bureau are just three organizations that keep data on international population characteristics. Local and state/province governments often keep track of their own jurisdictions. If your target area is an organization, you need to target your inquiry on the department that may keep these data. You may increase your chances of finding a corporation's data in the human resources or strategic planning departments. At the local church, this gets more difficult, but the church secretary or the church membership committee chair might know. Smaller, less formally organized organizations are less likely to easily produce the information you want. Do not be surprised, at this level, if no one is counting!

The benefits of searching for population for your presentation in government databases is that the information is often in the public domain. That means that often (you should always check!) you can use the information free of charge. A fringe benefit of the information age has been that many population graphics (such as the U.S. Census) appear on government websites. You may be able to download a graphic for your presentation from these sources.

Sociologist as Expert

Sociologists are not the only professionals who use demography in their work. Geographers, economists, planners of all kinds, market researchers, and policy analysts are just a few of the other professionals who use these factors to track human social life. In fact, many people who study the impact of population simply consider themselves to be demographers. This is a case in which a sociologist must broaden skills to include demography in order to be an expert.

Sociologists are trained to see the big picture. In this chapter, we have tried to show applied demography at successive levels of social organization: micro, meso, and macro. A professional demographer is a valuable team member. But much can be accomplished by an applied sociologist with a solid understanding of the basic population balancing equation and the formulas for measuring birth, death, and migration. Particularly advantageous is the sociologist's propensity to ask about the impact of demographic forces on the nature of social life. An applied sociologist adds value to interpreting the nature of a problem when he or she can get a client to understand the daily life result of demographic changes. The sociologist augments awareness when he or she asks the right demographic questions. What cultural and subcultural changes might occur as a result of population increase or change in population characteristics? What social systems need to be changed as a result of current or future demographic trends? What are the intended and unintended consequences of these changes? These are powerful questions that, when answered, provide more realistic solutions to problems.

▧ Case Study

There are many other demographic forces that influence social life. This book just gets you started. It gives you enough information to empower you to measure and use demography as an important factor in the sociological analysis of a setting. Now, let us return to a local level. A business in your community has decided to develop a plan for the next 10 years. One of the major concerns the company faces is a flow of trained personnel to conduct business. Your main contact in the company is the Vice President for Human Resources. She tells you that the company got its start in the 1950s. It experienced major expansion in the 1960s and 1970s with the addition of a large number of young college graduates in all of its major departments. The company has had steady financial growth and was able to weather the recession of the early 1980s without laying off any employees. The vice president goes on to tell you that the company has been a good place to work, and many people have held on to their jobs. Many of those employed in the 1960s and 1970s still remain. The company has provided good fringe benefits: health care, insurance, and retirement benefits. Wages have always been comparable with competing companies. Now, she wants you to look at the company's workforce and advise her of any strengths, weaknesses, opportunities, and threats that might emerge as a result of the composition of the company's workforce. You decide that your first step is to do a demographic analysis of the company.

Possible Solutions

Internal Background

1. Locate and gather all the demographic data available within the company.
   a. How big is the company (number of employees)?

  b. What is the nature of the company's growth since it began?

  c. What has been the nature of the company's growth in the past 5 years?

2. What are the likely demands for personnel growth in the company over the next 5 years?

Develop a Brief Demographic Profile of the Company

1. Look at the age of employees.

   a. What has happened to the average age of employees in the company over time? (Cross-tabulate the number of employees in each job classification level [education/skill level] by age group.)

   b. How many employees will be eligible to retire in the next 5 years? The next 10 years?

   c. If these employees leave the company, what impact will this have?

   d. What postretirement concerns face the company over the next 5 to 10 years?

2. Look at the sex and age of employees.

   a. Compare the sex ratio (number of men vs. number of women) in the company over its history.

   b. Demographically speaking, what does the most frequent employee look like with regard to age and sex at specific time periods in the company's history? What does this person look like now? What will this person look like in the future? (Cross-tabulate the number of employees in each job classification level [education/skill level] by sex.)

3. Construct a population pyramid for the company.

   a. What is happening to the proportion of men and women in the company?

   b. Will the company need to hire an increased number of younger women and men in the next 5 to 10 years? What impact would this have on company policy?

4. Determine the racial-ethnic diversity level in the workforce.

   a. What is happening to the proportion of ethnic and racial cultural groups in the company?

   b. What is the nature of the diversity profile now and in the future?

5. Create an ethnic, age, and gender profile for the workforce.

Determine the Corporate Culture

1. Through key informant interviews, focus groups, or surveys, determine the company way of life (consider interviewing senior management, staff/workers, and clients).

   a. To what degree does this culture reflect the current demographic composition of the company?

b. Will the changing company demographics that you have just outlined have any impact on the corporate culture?

c. What impact is likely? Do you anticipate a cultural change?

d. Outline the likely corporate cultural changes that are likely based on your demographic analysis.

External Background

1. Locate and gather all of the demographic data available in the target area from which the company has traditionally drawn its employees.
   a. What is the population of this area?
   b. What is the nature of this area's growth since the company's inception?
   c. What has been the nature of the area's growth in the past 5 years?
2. Consider immigration into and emigration from the area.
3. What is the likely available supply of personnel to the company over the next 5 to 10 years?

Develop a Brief Demographic Profile of the Target Area

1. Look at the population's age.
   a. What has happened to the average age of the population over time?
   b. What proportion is beyond retirement by age over the next 5 years? The next 10 years?
   c. What impact will this labor supply have on the company?
2. Look at the population's sex and age.
   a. Compare the sex ratio in the target area over the company's history.
   b. Demographically speaking, what does the most frequent person in the target area look like with regard to age and sex at specific time periods in the company's history? What does this person look like now? What will this person look like in the future? (Estimate and cross-tabulate the number of available employees in each job classification level [education/skill level] by sex.)
3. Construct a population pyramid for the area.
   a. What is happening to the proportion of men and women in the area?
   b. Demographically, will labor shortages occur?
4. Determine the racial-ethnic diversity level in the target area.
   a. What is happening to the proportion of ethnic and racial cultural groups in the target area?
   b. What is the nature of the diversity profile now and in the future?
5. Create an ethnic, age, and gender profile for the target area workforce.

Report the Findings

1. Outline the findings in bullets, that is, in a brief anecdotal summary like this:
   - Strengths
   - Weaknesses
   - Opportunities
   - Threats
2. Outline your recommendations for likely additions to the company's plan in bullets. Each of your recommendations should directly link to at least one of the categories above.

※ Exercises

Select a local organization that interests you. Clearly define the boundary of the organization. You could look at a city or a county, even a state. However, a smaller organization, such as your church or a local social agency, would be a good example and make analysis a little easier. You will need to get demographic data for the organization. Demographic variables include such items as sex, age, and race (and sometimes ethnicity).

1. Obtain the information at a number of different levels.

   - The total number of people in the organization for this year (or the most recent year).
   - The total number of people in the organization for years prior to this year (or the most recent year). If projections for the future are available (estimates of these factors in future years), get those also.
   - The number of people in the organization by each of the demographic variables listed above for this year (or the most recent year).
   - The number of people in the organization for each of these variables for years prior to this year. If projections for the future are available (estimates of these factors in future years), get those also.

2. Record the data in a tabular form so that you can compare it over time. Prepare two tables with these numbers in them. It will look something like Tables 10.1 and 10.2. Now, perform the calculations necessary

Table 10.1 Total Population of Organization X From Year 19?? to Year 20??

Total Population Estimates for	Years Prior 19xx	Years Prior 20xx	Most Recent Year Years After 19xx	Estimates for Years After 20xx
Count				
Percentage increase or decrease				

Table 10.2 Total Population of Organization X from 19?? to 20??

Demographic Variable	Years Prior 19xx	Years Prior 20xx	Most Recent Year Years After 19xx	Estimates for Years After 20xx
Age (count)				
Categories of age follow				
Age (percentage)				
Categories of age follow				
Sex (count)				
Female				
Male				
Sex (percentage)				
Female				
Male				
Race/ethnicity (count)				
Appropriate race categories here				
Race/Ethnicity (percentage)				
Appropriate race categories here				

to fill in the tables. You can do this by hand, by calculator, or in a computer spreadsheet.

3. Analyze the information. Consider the following:

- What is the size of the organization now?
- What has been happening to the overall size of the organization over time?
- What is the nature of the distribution of (the proportion of) each group now?
    1. Age?
    2. Sex?
    3. Race/ethnicity?

- What is the nature of the distribution of (the proportion of) each group over time?
  a. Age?
  b. Sex?
  c. Race/ethnicity?
- What is the estimated overall size of the organization in the future?
- What is the nature of the distribution of (the proportion of) each group in the future?
  1. Age?
  2. Sex?
  3. Race/Ethnicity?

4. Now, assess the reason that these changes happened. Why did these changes occur? Assess each of the following:

- Demographic factors: fertility, mortality, immigration, emigration, other?
- Social or organizational factors: culture/attitudes, family, economic, political, religious, educational, other?
- In short, what caused the population change?

Now, assess the impact. How have changing demographic factors influenced life in the organization? Personally or in a group, brainstorm this question. If evidence of impact is available, report it as well.

Complete the following table:

Population change: What happened?	Environment
Impact on each of the following up to the most recent date:	Physical surroundings
	Natural resources
What outcome?	Other
Impact on each of the following in the future:	Technology
	Presence of new
What outcome?	Amount
Organization:	Type
General structure?	Other
Family	Culture
Economic/financial	New ways of life
Government/management	Value changes
Education/training	Norms changed
Religion/esprit de corps	New beliefs

PART  III

Curtain Call

Appendix A
Putting It All Together

Now that you have learned some of the tricks of the trade, you are ready to put them all together. You have learned key sociological perspectives to view the situation. You have also identified different methodological techniques that can be applied to your analysis. You have a good understanding of the assortment of presentation tools available, and you have a good idea of which ones to use to best inform others of your findings. Most importantly, you are ready to apply your sociological skills to a wide variety of problems that you may be asked to investigate.

This appendix has been designed to help you develop a framework that can be used to evaluate a problem and present actionable results. This framework uses a number of questions that you can ask to best focus your analysis on the problem.

Defining the Problem

1. What is the problem you are investigating?
   a. How are others, such as your client, defining the problem?
   b. What is your initial perception of the problem?
2. Is the problem under investigation the real problem, or is it a symptom of other problems? (Be careful here! Many problems you face are just the tip of the iceberg, and there may be one or a number of factors below the surface that are causing this problem.)
3. What data or indicators are there to show that the problem really exists?
   a. How will you access the data? Does it already exist? Will you have to perform primary research?
   b. How reliable and accurate are the data and indicators?

Analyzing the Structure

1. What is going on in the social environment?
   a. What events, expected or unexpected, are affecting the structure?

    b. Has the social environment been relatively stable, or has it been in transition?

2. How would you define the social structure?
    a. What are the key structural factors affecting the situation?
    b. How do the individuals involved define and view the structure?

3. What are the key roles and statuses?
    a. What are the group-defined roles and statuses?
    b. Are there additional roles and statuses that have emerged?
    c. How different are the emergent roles and statuses from those defined by the group?

4. What are the group's strategic plans and objectives?
    a. What are the defined mission, goals, objectives, and outcomes?
    b. How does the group define success in each of these areas?
    c. How does the group measure this success?
    d. How successful has the group been in each of these strategic areas?

Analyzing the Process

1. What are the key processes working in the group?
    a. Are these processes different from what the group has stated them to be?
    b. How well do the processes support the strategic directives of the group?
    c. Are there any clearly observable "disconnects" in the process?

2. What are the key group norms?
    a. Do the norms support the existing structure?
    b. Do individuals clearly understand the norms of the group?
    c. Have new norms emerged?

How Is the Organization Defined?

1. How is the group structured?
    a. Does the existing structure of the group differ from the individuals' perceptions of it?
    b. Are there any obvious disconnects in the stated and real structures?

2. Does the group share an agreed upon culture?
    a. Are the members familiar with this culture?
    b. Do the members adhere to or follow this culture?
    c. Are there subcultures present in the group?

Who Are the Leaders?

1. Who are the group's defined leaders?

a. How did these leaders obtain their positions of leadership?
b. How long have these individuals been in their leadership positions?
c. Have these leaders formed a coalition?
d. How do the members interact with the leaders?
2. How do the leaders lead?
a. What type of authority structure is used? Is it authoritarian (chain of command), or is it egalitarian (coaching)?
b. What is the leadership style? Is it instrumental, expressive, or a combination of the two?
3. How does the membership respond to the leadership authority and style?
a. Are there other, unspecified leaders in the group?
b. Does the membership support the leadership style and structure?
4. How effective is the current leadership?
a. Does the leadership meet the stated goals and objectives?
b. How does the membership rate the leaders on their effectiveness?

What About Cultural Differences?

1. Are there ethnic and cultural differences in the group?
a. How do these differences affect the group?
b. Are the members aware of the cultural differences?
c. Do they understand the cultural differences?
2. Are the cultural differences causing misunderstandings or problems within the group?
3. What is being done (if anything) to effectively use these differences?
a. Are differences encouraged?
b. Is cultural information shared and integrated into group culture?
c. Are there opportunities for cross-cultural training for leaders and members?

How Does the Group Adapt to Change?

1. Is the group currently in a state of transition or change?
a. How is the group defining the change?
b. How is the group responding to the change?
c. How is the change affecting the group's behavior?
2. What are the key trends affecting the group?
a. Are these trends microscopic, mesoscopic, or macroscopic?
b. How are these trends linked?
c. How does the group view and respond to these trends?

What About Deviant Behavior?

1. Are there any acts or behaviors that deviate from the group's norms?
   a. Is this deviance sanctioned or accepted by the group?
   b. Has the deviance become the norm for the group?
2. How are the acts of deviance affecting the group?
   a. Is the deviance a response to norms that are perceived to be out of date or nonproductive?
   b. Are these acts of deviance bringing about change in the group?

What About the Unexpected?

1. Are there, or have there been, unexpected events that have caused changes or disruptions to the group?
   a. What were these unexpected events?
   b. What was the impact of these events on the group?
   c. How did the group view the events and their impact?
2. How is or has the group responded to the event and its impact?
3. How much change, if any, has the event had on the strategic direction of the group?

What About Demographic Challenges?

1. What is the demographic makeup of the group?
2. Has the demographic composition of the group changed recently?
3. What has been the impact of this change?
4. What will the group need to do or change in order to meet the changing demographics?

The above questions should be viewed only as benchmark questions to get you to start thinking about the problem you are investigating. Your actual analysis will use these questions to generate many more. At their basic level, the above questions should give you both structure and a process to complete your analysis. As you proceed with your investigation, you will want to develop your own more thorough and specific line of questioning and analysis. Good hunting!

Appendix B
The Ethical Sociologist

All scientists, especially those researching human attitudes and behaviors, must ground their thoughts and actions in a strong ethical foundation. No research, be it pure or applied, is worth the cost of harming the individual or individuals being studied. Ethics are not just a set of rules or regulations on dealing with human subjects; they are part of the scientist's own personal value system and way of life. Good ethics are not only morally correct, they are part and parcel of good research and good sociological applications.

As a sociologist, you will come into contact with potential ethical issues at a number of different levels. First of all, in the role of sociologist, you will be asked to deal with issues of ethics in both your research and your practice. Research can be full of potential ethical pitfalls if the sociologist is not prepared for them. For example, the subject of the research may be in areas that are illegal activities in a society (e.g., drugs, crime, abuse). As the researcher, you must decide how you will deal with these subjects as you study them. Remember that committing an illegal act in the name of science is not good research, and you are liable for the act you committed. Many times, unethical practices occur when the researcher does not take the time to do his or her homework before beginning the research. Understanding the dynamics of the social event or phenomenon you are going to study will help you to identify potential problems before they have a chance to happen.

Once the research is complete, the sociologist must then decide how to turn the findings into useable applications. Once again, a strong ethical foundation must be at the heart of this process. Although research findings should never be intentionally misrepresented, the researcher must be careful to ensure that the findings do not harm the respondents or individuals associated with them. Once again, the researcher must be prepared to make an ethical decision on what to do with the results. Remember, this is serious business. Individuals have been harmed in the name of research, and researchers have gone to jail for refusing to report results that would have left the respondents injured or harmed. The best way to stay out of this situation is to brainstorm all possible outcomes of the research and results before entering into it. This will allow you to build safeguards into the actual research and to discuss with the client all of the potential risks involved.

Dealing with the client is the second area in which the sociologist must maintain ethical standards. Most clients are in need of information, and that is why they hired you to gather it. Many of these clients have previously conceived notions on what they want the results to be. Not only is this poor research, but it is also unethical. The researcher must deal with the client in an ethical and legal manner. The client must understand that you will perform the research in the most unbiased way possible, and that you will not be swayed in your judgment because of their wants. This needs to be discussed diplomatically but firmly with the client before you enter into a contract to do the research.

During the research, you must make sure that the client does not require changes that would potentially harm respondents or destroy the privacy that you guaranteed them. Once the research has ended, you must try your hardest to make sure that the client uses the raw data and your report in an ethical manner. This is easier said than done. In most cases, the data belong to the client. This is why it is important to make sure that the clients understand that only good ethical research will solve their needs. Not only will the information be more accurate, but also both of you will be less likely to face a lawsuit or, in some cases, a criminal charge.

A third area of concern is the ethics of the subjects being studied. Respondents have been known to lie and falsify information during research. As a researcher, you will want to make sure that checks and balances are placed throughout the research to ensure that chances for these types of problems are minimized. Also, if you spot a respondent committing an unethical act, it is your moral and professional obligation to remove him or her from the research. If you observe or if the respondent tells you that he or she is committing a criminal act, it is your legal responsibility to report it.

Many of these problems can be controlled if the researcher maintains an ethically correct stance throughout all aspects of the research project. If you are doing research in a university or agency setting, you may be required to present your research proposal to a committee that has been called together to evaluate potential harm to human subjects. Make sure that this committee understands the potential harmful effects, if any, that may happen because of your research and what you plan on doing to safeguard the respondents and researchers from these potential problems. If you are doing the research outside of a government or university setting that does not require the approval of a human subjects committee, you should discuss the research with your colleagues, allowing them the opportunity to review your proposal and then discuss with you their concerns and suggestions on how to make the research as safe as possible.

Finally, as the researcher, you have the moral obligation to protect those individuals whom you are studying. There may be times when your professionalism and ethics will force you to turn down or walk away from research projects that you feel are less than ethical. This is acceptable behavior and the proper thing to do. Put yourself in the role of the respondent in your research, and if you have problems or feel threatened by the research, then there is also a chance that your respondents will feel the same way.

PART

Taking the
Show on the Road

Appendix C
A Basic Toolkit for Applied Sociologists

Throughout this book, we have tried to connect sociology to a variety of practical pursuits. Below, we have listed some techniques or concepts that we believe belong in your toolkit. For each, you will find a brief annotation (a reason why you need it or what it is), a practical how-to reference, and at least one URL—website—to consult. We end the list with some assistance in getting a job!

⊠ Applied Demography

Understanding, measuring, and applying changing population forces are rich and valuable skills. Applied sociologists need a basic understanding of demography.

> **Helpful Reference:** Population Reference Bureau. (1997). *Population handbook U.S. edition* (4th ed.). Washington, DC: Author.

URLs:
 http://www.prb.org/ (great overall access to population data)
 http://www.demographics.com/ (American demographics, and some great marketing and general interest uses of demography)

⊠ Applied Sociology

One way to view applied sociology is "any use (often client-centered) of the sociological perspective and/or its tools in the understanding of, intervention in and/or the enhancement of human social life." Applied sociology is active and creative.

Helpful Reference: Steele, S., & Iutcovich J. (Eds.). (1997). *Directions in applied sociology: Presidential addresses of the Society for Applied Sociology 1985-1995*. Arnold, MD: Society for Applied Sociology.

URL:

   http://www.appliedsoc.org

⧨ Applied Tools

The more tools, the better—when you are in the field working with clients, you will want to provide the most rigorous strategies for problem identification and solution. Learning new tools and skills, or converting ones you learned for another purpose to applied settings, is valuable.

Helpful Reference: Bickman, L., & Rog, D. (Eds.). (1998). *Handbook of applied social research methods*. Thousand Oaks, CA: Sage.

URL:

   http://www.sagepub.com/sagepage/search.html

⧨ Business Plan

Eventually, you will need to assist a client (you might need to do this for your own consulting business) in writing a business plan. You need to know the basics. Bookstores have dozens of how-to books on this one!

Helpful Reference: King, J. (1994). *Business plans to game plans: A practical system for turning strategies into action*. Santa Monica, CA: Merritt.

URLs:

   http://www.ecodev.state.mo.us/mbac/busplan/default.htm
   http://zeta.is.tcu.edu/blobert/vle/business.html

◙ Continuous Improvement Models

Whether it is total quality management or continuous improvement, applied sociologists will find opportunities for improving organizations and processes. A variety of techniques are needed here: brainstorming, nominal group technique, fishbone diagrams, and basic problem solving. Whether it is brainstorming, benchmarking, Pareto, or fishbone charts, you will need a guide on how to do these basic problem exploration and solving strategies.

> **Helpful Reference:** GOAL/QPC. (1994). *The memory jogger II: A pocket guide of tools for continuous improvement and effective planning.* Methuen, MA: Author.

URL:

http://www.usaor.net/users/thall3/Contimp.htm

◙ Creative Problem Solving

Applied sociologists are called upon not only to identify problems, but also to recommend solutions. Simple strategies for producing creative solutions are essential.

> **Helpful Reference:** Higgins, J. (1994). *101 creative problem solving techniques: The handbook of new ideas for business.* Winter Park, FL: New Management Publishing.

URLs:

http://www.changedynamics.com/samples/probsolv.htm (a good template for creative problem solving)

http://www.changedynamics.com/samples/samples.htm (a homepage with several related templates)

◙ Focus Groups

Initially the work of a sociologist, Robert K. Merton, this qualitative technique, which uses trained moderators for data gathering in small groups, has become a modern workhorse. Knowledge of focus groups is a basic tool.

> **Helpful Reference:** Krueger, R. (1994). *Focus groups: A practical guide to applied research* (2nd ed.). Thousand Oaks, CA: Sage.

URL:
> http://www.gwbssw.wustl.edu/csd/evaluation/fgroups/
> fghowto.html

ℳ Futures Research and Analysis

Studying the future is a natural outgrowth of the tools and per-spectives of applied sociology.

> **Helpful Reference:** Cornish, E. (1977). *The study of the future.* Bethesda, MD: World Future Society.

URL:
> http://www.wfs.org/wfs/index.htm

ℳ Indicators and Trends

Getting an overview of important indicators and trends is often essential.

> **Helpful Reference:** Davis, J., & Smith, T. (1991). *The NORC General Social Survey user's guide.* Thousand Oaks, CA: Sage.

URLs:
> http://www.clark.net/pub/ssteele/home.htm
> http://www.icpsr.umich.edu/gss/home.htm

ℳ Leadership

Sooner or later, an applied sociologist will run into the need to advise clients on decisions for their future. Thus, you will find yourself becoming a leader or helping to create leaders. Workshops on leadership and making tough decisions are part of this.

> **Helpful References:** Bennis, W. (1989). *On becoming a leader.* Reading, MA: Addison-Wesley.
> Bennis, W., & Goldsmith, J. (1994). *Learning to lead: A workbook on becoming a leader.* Reading, MA: Addison-Wesley.

URL:

> http://www.exen.com/CCLfr.html

⧠ Needs Assessment

Determining and substantiating need for a change, project, or program is a valuable applied skill. Understanding the method for doing this type of work is an essential skill.

> **Helpful Reference:** Witkin, B. R., & Altschuld, J. W. (1995). *Planning and conducting needs assessment.* Thousand Oaks, CA: Sage.

URL: The Cultural Reconstruction and Development (CURED) has produced some excellent guidelines for planning and development.

> http://star.hsrc.ac.za/socdyn/cguide.html#Strategic

⧠ Organizations

Change, restructuring, and training within organizations provide clear opportunities to use your sociology.

> **Helpful Reference:** Morgan, G. (1996). *Images of organization.* Thousand Oaks, CA: Sage.

URL:

> http://www.yorku.ca/faculty/academic/gmorgan/index.html

▨ Making Presentations

Applied sociologists rarely read papers to their audiences! Become familiar with a variety of presentation skills. Learn to stand before an audience and deliver your information.

> **Helpful Reference:** Torres, R., Presell, H., & Piontek, M. (1996). *Evaluation strategies for communicating and reporting: Enhancing learning in organizations.* Thousand Oaks, CA: Sage.

URL:

http://www.presentec.com/files/articles/articles.html

▨ Process Reengineering

Get a handle on the vocabulary here. Sociologists have called this restructuring. You will find reengineering familiar and a good place for applied work.

> **Helpful Reference:** Hammer, M., & Stanton, S. (1995). *The reengineering revolution.* New York: HarperCollins.

URL:

http://www.reengineering.com/

▨ Program Evaluation

Deciding whether or not a program, project, training, or plan works is an important application of sociology. Providing recommendations for program improvement and change requires a broad toolkit.

> **Helpful Reference:** Wholey, J., Hatry, H., & Newcomb, K. (Eds.). (1994). *Handbook of practical program evaluation.* San Francisco: Jossey-Bass.

URLs:

http://www.eval.org/index.html
http://www.eval.org/progeval.html

ꙮ Qualitative Methods

The academic conflict may rage over quantitative versus qualitative methods, but as an applied sociologist, you are looking for the best tools to do the job. These tools may be quantitative and/or qualitative. Make sure your toolkit includes qualitative methods.

> **Helpful Reference:** Denzin, N., & Lincoln, Y. (1994). *Handbook of qualitative research.* Thousand Oaks, CA: Sage.

URL:
> http://www.siu.edu/hawkes/methods.html#qualitative

ꙮ General Research Methods

There is no substitute for a solid understanding of social research methods if you plan to be an applied sociologist. This, combined with creativity and rigor, will increase your toolkit!

> **Helpful Reference:** Babbie, E. (1997). *The practice of social research* (8th ed.). Belmont, CA: Wadsworth/ITP.

URL: Roland Hawkes of Southern Illinois University is to be commended for this great site! It's a "soup-to-nuts" overview of important links in teaching and doing social science research.

> http://www.siu.edu/hawkes/methods.html

ꙮ Strategic Planning

Strategic planning is a good area for applied sociologists. Learning to assist in the development of organizational plans is a logical extension of the craft of sociology.

> **Helpful Reference:** Barry, B. (1997). *Strategic planning workbook for non-profit organizations* (revised and updated). St. Paul, MN: Amherst H. Wilder Foundation.

URLs: The Cultural Reconstruction and Development (CURED) has produced some excellent guidelines for planning and development.

> http://star.hsrc.ac.za/socdyn/cguide.html#Strategic
> http://www.colybrand.com/clc/gov/stratpln.html

◎ Survey Research

Survey research is a basic tool for applied sociologists. Learn how to do it well.

> **Helpful Reference:** Fink, A., & Kosecoff, J. (1985). *How to conduct surveys: A step-by-step guide.* Beverly Hills, CA: Sage.

URL:
> http://www.geom.umn.edu/docs/snell/chance/teaching_aids/
> survey/survey.html

◎ Getting a Job

Face it—applied sociologists with a bachelor's degree are in the same job market with other BA-level people from other disciplines. Basic job-hunting skills are essential. Learn to write a resume and job hunt.

> **Helpful Reference:** Mobley, C., Steele, S., & Rowell, K. (1997). *Getting a head start on your career as an applied sociologist: A workbook for job seekers in sociology.* Arnold, MD: Society for Applied Sociology.

URLs:
> http://www.monster.com
> http://www.starthere.com/jobs/
> http://www.espan.com
> http://www.Careercity.com

References

Ackoff, R. (1981). *Creating the corporate future*. New York: John Wiley.

Babbie, E. (1994). *The sociological spirit* (2nd ed.). Belmont, CA: Wadsworth/ITP.

Barry, B. (1986). *Strategic planning workbook for nonprofit organizations*. St. Paul, MN: Amherst H. Wilder Foundation.

Bell, D. (1973). *The coming of post-industrial society*. New York: Basic Books.

Bennis, W. (1989). *On becoming a leader*. Reading, MA: Addison-Wesley.

Bennis, W., & Goldsmith, J. (1994). *Learning to lead: A workbook on becoming a leader*. Reading, MA: Addison-Wesley.

Berger, P., & Luckmann, T. (1966). *The social construction of reality*. Garden City, NY: Doubleday.

Cantor, D., Comber, M., & Uzzell, D. L. (1989). *Football in its place: An environmental psychology of football grounds*. London: Routledge.

Cooley, C. H. (1902). *Human nature and the social order*. New York: Scribner.

Crosby, P. (1996). *The absolutes of leadership*. San Diego, CA: Pfeiffer & Company.

Danzger, H. M. (1975). Validating conflict data. *Amerian Sociological Review, 40*(5), 570-584.

Durkheim, E. (1951). *Suicide: A study in sociology* (J. A. Spaulding & G. Simpson, Trans.). New York: Free Press.

Goodstein, L., Nolan, T., & Pfeiffer, J. W. (1993). *Applied strategic planning: How to develop a plan that really works*. New York: McGraw-Hill.

Hall, R. (1987). *Organizations: Structures, processes & outcomes*. Englewood Cliffs, NJ: Prentice Hall.

Hawley, A. (1971). *Urban society: An ecological approach*. New York: Ronald Press.

Hunt, V. D. (1992). *Quality in America: How to implement a competitive quality program*. Homewood, IL: Business One Irwin.

LeBon, G. (1879). *The crowd: A study of the popular mind*. London: T. F. Unwin.

Marx, G., & McAdam, D. (1994). *Collective behavior and social movements*. Englewood Cliffs, NJ: Prentice Hall.

McPhail, C., & Miller, D. L. (1973). The assembling process: A theoretical and empirical examination. *American Sociological Review, 38*, 721-735.

McPhail, C., & Wohlstein, R. (1983). Individual and collective behaviors within gatherings, demonstrations, and riots. *American Review of Sociology, 9*, 579-600.

Mead, G. H. (1934). *Mind, self and society* (C. W. Morris, Ed.). Chicago: University of Chicago Press.

Merton, R. (1968). *Social theory and social structure* (2nd ed.). New York: Free Press.

Miller, D. (1985). *Introduction to collective behavior*. Belmont, CA: Wadsworth.

Patton, M. (1990). *Qualitative evaluation and research methods* (2nd ed.). Newbury Park, CA: Sage.

Peters, T. (1988). *Thriving on chaos: A handbook for a management revolution.* New York: Knopf.

Population Reference Bureau. (1997). *Population handbook* (4th U.S. ed.). Washington, DC: Author.

Ritzer, G. (1996). *The McDonaldization of society* (Rev. ed.). Thousand Oaks, CA: Pine Forge.

Rossi, P., & Freeman, H. (1989). *Evaluation: A systematic approach* (4th ed.). Newbury Park, CA: Sage.

Schein, E. (1992). *Organizational culture & leadership* (2nd ed.). San Francisco: Jossey-Bass.

Scriven, M. (1967). The methodology of evaluation. In R. W. Tyler, R. M. Gagne, & M. Scriven (Eds.), *Perspectives of curriculum evaluation* (pp. 39-83). Chicago: Rand McNally.

Scriven, M. (1991). *Evaluation thesaurus.* Newbury Park, CA: Sage.

Shostak, A. (1988). Applied sociology in the year 2000: Possible impacts of technology. *Journal of Applied Sociology, 5,* 33-40.

Simmel, G. (1902). The number of members as determining the sociological form of the group. *American Journal of Sociology, 8,* 1-46, 158-196.

Smelser, N. J. (1962). *Theory of collective behavior.* New York: Free Press.

Steele, S. (1996). Five steps to an evaluation: The Five D's. *Social Insight: Knowledge at Work, 1,* 52.

Turner, R. H., & Killian, L. (1957). *Collective behavior.* Englewood Cliffs, NJ: Prentice Hall.

Ventura, S. J., Martin, J. A., Curtin, S. C., & Mathews, T. J. (1997). Report of final natality statistics, 1995. *Monthly vital statistics report* (Vol. 45, No. 11, Supp.). Hyattsville, MD: National Center for Health Statistics.

Ward, L. (1907). The establishment of sociology. *Publications of the American Sociological Society, 1*(1), 9.

Weber, L. (1995). *The analysis of social problems.* Boston: Allyn and Bacon.

Wenger, D. E. (1978). Community responses to disaster: Functional and structural alterations. In E. L. Quarantelli (Ed.), *Disaster, theory and research* (pp. 17-49). Beverly Hills, CA: Sage.

Witkin, B. R., & Altschuld, J. W. (1995). *Planning and conducting needs assessment.* Thousand Oaks, CA: Sage.

Index

About the Authors

William (Bill) J. Hauser, PhD, is currently Manager of Business Development and Research at The Little Tikes Company (a division of Rubbermaid Inc.), where he is in charge of business intelligence, market research, strategic planning, and new business development. Over the years, he has held numerous applied sociology positions, including being a desegregation analyst for the St. Louis (MO) Board of Education; a senior research associate for a military contractor; and numerous research, strategic planning, and development positions at Rubbermaid. Dr. Hauser is currently an adjunct professor of sociology at the University of Akron. He is also the president (1999) of the Society for Applied Sociology.

AnneMarie Scarisbrick-Hauser, PhD, is Associate Director of the Institute for Policy Studies at the University of Akron, where she is in charge of the Urban and Policy Research Division. In this role, she is responsible for managing the university's community research partnership program and its survey research center. Over the past 10 years, she has directed more than 100 research projects for businesses, social agencies, the media, and the university. A sociologist, Dr. Scarisbrick-Hauser is also an adjunct professor in the Department of Political Science at the University of Akron and has taught on both the elementary and secondary school levels in Ireland. Currently, she is working with numerous state and community groups in the areas of strategic planning and evaluation.

Stephen F. Steele, PhD, has applied sociology's concepts and tools for more than two decades. As a teacher, practitioner, and leader, he has been an advocate for understanding the practical value of the application of social science. For more than 25 years, he has integrated teaching and the development of applied sociology at Anne Arundel Community College. In 1978, he was one of the founders of the Center for the Study of Local Issues (CSLI), which works locally to enhance the problem-solving value of sociology and social science, and nationally to promote the applied research center as a model vehicle for local research. In the 1990s, Dr. Steele answered the call for leadership in the Society for Applied Sociology, serving as vice president in 1990 and president in 1992-1993. Dr. Steele and his wife, Cindy, maintain Applied Data Associates, Inc., a small research and consulting partnership created to develop research, planning, and evaluation products and procedures. Today, he continues his work at Anne Arundel Community College and has extended his teaching efforts to the graduate education level in the Human Resources and Organizational Development Program (in the Division of Business) at the Johns Hopkins University School of Continuing Studies.